교과서 필수 문법으로 익히는 영어 문장 쓰기

WRITING
BUILDER

3

KB014129

WRITING BUILDER 3

지은이	NE능률 영어교육연구소
선임연구원	김동숙
연구원	양빈나 김은환 김은향 황선영
영문 교열	Patrick Ferraro, Amanda Brockus, Daniel Baum
디자인	윤혜정 윤성준 김지연
내지 일러스트	끌레몽 윤예지
표지 일러스트	김나영
맥편집	김재민
영업	한기영, 이경구, 박인규, 정철교, 김남준, 김남형, 이우현
마케팅	박혜선, 고유진, 김여진

Copyright©2013 by NE Neungyule, Inc.

All rights reserved. No part of this publication may be reproduced, stored in a retrieval system, or transmitted in any form or by any means, electronic, mechanical, photocopying, recording, or otherwise, without the prior permission of the copyright owner.

· 본 교재의 독창적인 내용에 대한 일체의 무단 전재·모방은 법률로 금지되어 있습니다.

· 파본은 구매처에서 교환 가능합니다.

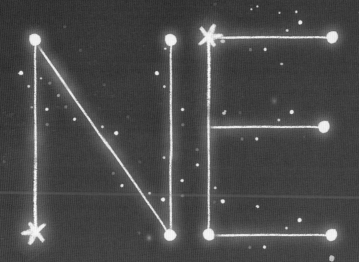

NE능률이 미래를 그립니다.

교육에 대한 큰 꿈을 품고 시작한 NE능률
처음 품었던 그 꿈을 잊지 않고 40년이 넘는 시간 동안 한 길만을 걸어왔습니다.

이제 NE능률이 앞으로 나아가야 할 길을 그려봅니다.
'평범한 열 개의 제품보다 하나의 탁월한 제품'이라는
변치 않는 철학을 바탕으로 진정한 배움의 가치를 알리는
NE능률이 교육의 미래를 열어가겠습니다.

NE 능
률

www.neungyule.com

NE능률의 모든 교재가 한 곳에 - 엔이 북스

NE_Books

www.nebooks.co.kr ▼

NE능률의 유초등 교재부터 중고생 참고서,
토익·토플 수험서와 일반 영어까지!
PC는 물론 태블릿 PC, 스마트폰으로 언제 어디서나
NE능률의 교재와 다양한 학습 자료를 만나보세요.

✓ 필요한 부가 학습 자료 바로 찾기
✓ 주요 인기 교재들을 한눈에 확인
✓ 나에게 딱 맞는 교재를 찾아주는 스마트 검색
✓ 함께 보면 좋은 교재와 다음 단계 교재 추천
✓ 회원 가입, 교재 후기 작성 등 사이트 활동 시 NE Point 적립

영어교과서 리딩튜터 능률보카 빠른독해 바른독해 수능만만 월등한 개념 수학 유형더블 토마토토익 NE 클래스
NE_Build & Grow   NE_Times   NE_Kids(굿잡,상상수프)   NE_능률 주니어랩   아이챌린지

건강한
배움의 즐거움

NE 능률

서문

최근 우리나라 영어 교육의 가장 큰 특징은 실용 영어의 중시와 함께
말하기, 쓰기와 같은 표현 영어를 강조하는 방향으로 변화하고 있다는
점입니다. 근래에 들어 말하기, 쓰기 능력을 평가하려는 시도가
활발해지고 있는 것도 이러한 변화의 일환입니다. 특히 쓰기는 인터넷과
이메일 등 글을 통한 세계와의 접촉이 활발해지는 상황에서 자기 생각을
정확하게 표현하기 위해 반드시 길러야 하는 능력입니다.
쓰기 실력을 향상시키기 위해서는 논리력, 구성력, 표현력 등 여러 가지
능력을 연마해야 합니다. 하지만 우선 영어 문장을 제대로 쓰기 위해
문장의 구조 및 영문법을 이해한 후 이를 바탕으로 충분히 연습해야
합니다. 이에 Writing Builder는 자주 쓰는 문형 및 문법을 익혀 이를
토대로 문장을 써보는 단계적인 학습을 통해 쓰기의 기본기를 탄탄히
쌓을 수 있도록 구성하였습니다. 또한 실생활과 밀접한 상황과 실용문을
통해 영어 문장 쓰기에 친근하게 접근할 수 있도록 하고 풍부한 연습
문제로 영작에 익숙해질 수 있도록 하였습니다.
Writing Builder를 통해 여러분은 영어 문장 쓰는 것에 자신감을
갖고, 나아가 자기 생각을 글로 표현할 수 있게 될 것입니다. Writing
Builder가 영어로 글쓰기의 기본을 쌓고자 할 때는 물론, 쓰기 서술형
평가를 준비할 때에도 소중한 디딤돌이 되었으면 합니다.

목차

구성과 특징

영어 문장 쓰기 핵심 Point 정리

문장 쓰기의 기본을 다지는 데 필요한 영어 문장 구조와 문법 사항을 간단명료하게 설명했습니다. 실용적인 예문을 제시하여 한 눈에 보기 쉽게 정리하였습니다.

추가 문법 사항 정리

핵심 Point와 함께 알아 두면 좋은 문법 사항을 정리해 두었습니다.

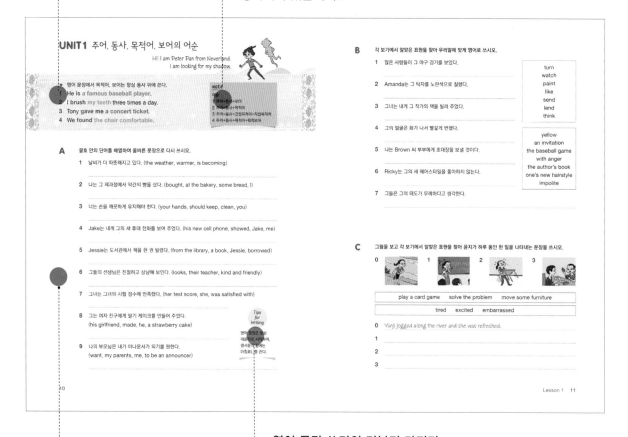

영어 문장 쓰기의 기본기 다지기

영어 문장 쓰기 실력을 향상시키는 데 필요한 기본적인 기술을 간략하게 설명하였습니다. 이를 통해 좀 더 정확한 문장을 쓸 수 있도록 하였습니다.

다양한 문제 유형을 통한 핵심 Point 연습

다양한 형태의 쓰기 문제를 통해 앞서 학습한 문장 구조 및 문법 사항의 이해도를 점검하고 문장 쓰기의 기초를 마련할 수 있도록 하였습니다.

연습 문제로 핵심 사항 정리

다양하고 심화된 연습 문제로 앞서 학습한 언어 표현과 쓰기 기술을
복습하고, 문장 쓰기에 익숙해질 수 있도록 하였습니다.

영어로 우리말 표현하기

완전한 문장을 직접 써 봄으로써 우리말을 영어로 표현하는 데
자신감을 키울 수 있도록 하였습니다.

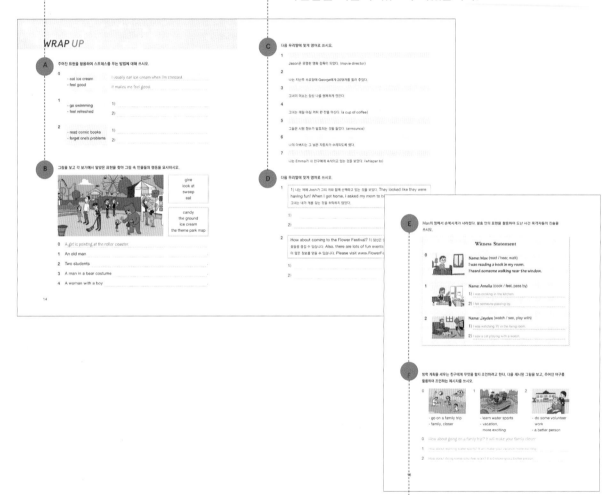

실용문과 서술형 평가 문제로 응용력 기르기

앞서 학습한 표현을 활용하여 일기, 이메일, 광고문 등의 실용문을
완성해 보고, 서술형 평가와 유사한 문제를 풀어봄으로써 응용력을
기를 수 있도록 하였습니다.

필수 문장 표현 익히기

사용 빈도가 높은 문장 패턴을 선별하여 실생활에서 자주 쓰이는 문장 표현에 익숙해질 수 있도록 하였습니다.

어휘 복습하기

Lesson별 중요 어휘를 복습하고 암기할 수 있도록 하였습니다.

Useful Patterns for Writing 1

★ 주어+means ~: ~는 …을 의미한다
His family means everything to him.

★ Please let me ~: 제가 ~하게 해 주세요
Please let me buy you dinner this time.

1 친구가 된다는 것은 서로를 믿는다는 것을 의미한다. (*trust: 믿다)

2 제가 당신과 함께 가도록 해 주세요.

3 많은 문화에서 깨진 거울은 불운을 의미한다.

4 제가 당신의 휴대 전화를 사용하도록 해 주세요.

5 어른이 된다는 것은 너의 행동들에 책임을 지는 것을 의미한다. (*responsibility: 책임)

6 당신의 이메일 주소를 제게 알려 주세요.

7 성공이 돈을 많이 버는 것을 의미하지는 않는다.

8 제 상황을 설명하게 해 주세요.

9 빨간색은 중국인에게 부와 행운을 의미한다. (*fortune: 부(富))

10 당신의 최종 결정을 제게 알려 주세요. (*final: 최종의)

LESSON 1

brush one's teeth 이를 닦다
comfortable 편안한
borrow 빌리다
be satisfied with ~에 만족하다
score 점수
announcer 아나운서, 방송 진행자
lend 빌려 주다
author 작가, 저자
anger 화, 분노
invitation 초대장

behavior 행동
impolite 무례한
refreshed (기분이) 상쾌한
embarrassed 당황스러운, 난처한
furniture 가구

excited 신이 난
perm 파마하다
repair 고치다, 수리하다
fire 발사하다
steal 훔치다

sweep 쓸다
floor 바닥
shake 흔들리다, 흔들다
badly 심하게, 몹시
fall down 넘어지다

stressed 스트레스를 받는
point at ~을 가리키다
costume 의상
director 감독, 책임자
announce 발표하다, 알리다

whisper 속삭이다
take a walk 산책하다
information 정보
witness 목격자
statement 진술

pass by (옆을) 지나가다
trip 여행
water sports 수상 스포츠
vacation 방학, 휴가
volunteer 자원봉사자

LESSON 2

wake up 깨우다
practice 연습하다
have a cold 감기에 걸리다
remind 상기시키다
already 이미, 벌써

full 배부른, 가득한
take a shower 샤워하다
ring (전화기) 울리다
trust 믿다, 신뢰하다
lift 들어 올리다

boring 지루한
fall asleep 잠들다
catch up with ~을 따라잡다
festival 축제
rice 쌀, 밥

stew 스튜
contact 연락하다
mentor 멘토, 충실한 조언자
refund 환불(금)
necklace 목걸이

earring 귀걸이
cheerful 쾌활한, 신이 나는
take part in ~에 참가하다
palm 손바닥
display 전시

turn off ~을 끄다
flash 동작시
take a picture 사진을 찍다
treat 다루다, 취급하다
with care 조심히여

stretch 뻗다, 스트레칭 하다
go camping 캠핑 가다
toothache 치통
terrible 형편없는, 끔찍한
burn 태다, 불에 타다

tongue 혀
hole 구멍
go on a picnic 소풍 가다
broken 고장 난
sneakers 운동화

SECTION 1

SENTENCE STRUCTURE

LESSON 1

문장의 기본

brush one's teeth	behavior	sweep	whisper
comfortable	impolite	floor	take a walk
borrow	refreshed	shake	information
be satisfied with	embarrassed	badly	witness
score	furniture	fall down	statement
announcer	excited	stressed	pass by
lend	perm	point at	trip
author	repair	costume	water sports
anger	fire	director	vacation
invitation	steal	announce	volunteer

UNIT1 주어, 동사, 목적어, 보어의 어순

Hi! I am Peter Pan from Neverland.
I am looking for my shadow.

★ 영어 문장에서 목적어, 보어는 항상 동사 뒤에 쓴다.
1 He **is** a famous baseball player.
2 I **brush** my teeth three times a day.
3 Tony **gave me** a concert ticket.
4 We **found** the chair comfortable.

note
어순
1 주어+동사+보어
2 주어+동사+목적어
3 주어+동사+간접목적어+직접목적어
4 주어+동사+목적어+목적보어

A 괄호 안의 단어를 배열하여 올바른 문장으로 다시 쓰시오.

1 날씨가 더 따뜻해지고 있다. (the weather, warmer, is becoming)

2 나는 그 제과점에서 약간의 빵을 샀다. (bought, at the bakery, some bread, I)

3 너는 손을 깨끗하게 유지해야 한다. (your hands, should keep, clean, you)

4 Jake는 내게 그의 새 휴대 전화를 보여 주었다. (his new cell phone, showed, Jake, me)

5 Jessie는 도서관에서 책을 한 권 빌렸다. (from the library, a book, Jessie, borrowed)

6 그들의 선생님은 친절하고 상냥해 보인다. (looks, their teacher, kind and friendly)

7 그녀는 그녀의 시험 점수에 만족했다. (her test score, she, was satisfied with)

8 그는 여자 친구에게 딸기 케이크를 만들어 주었다.
(his girlfriend, made, he, a strawberry cake)

9 나의 부모님은 내가 아나운서가 되기를 원한다.
(want, my parents, me, to be an announcer)

Tips for Writing

영어 문장은 항상 대문자로 시작하며, 평서문의 끝에는 마침표(.)를 쓴다.

B 각 보기에서 알맞은 표현을 찾아 우리말에 맞게 영어로 쓰시오.

1 많은 사람들이 그 야구 경기를 보았다.

_____

2 Amanda는 그 탁자를 노란색으로 칠했다.

_____

3 그녀는 내게 그 작가의 책을 빌려 주었다.

_____

4 그의 얼굴은 화가 나서 빨갛게 변했다.

_____

5 나는 Brown 씨 부부에게 초대장을 보낼 것이다.

_____

6 Ricky는 그의 새 헤어스타일을 좋아하지 않는다.

_____

7 그들은 그의 태도가 무례하다고 생각한다.

_____

| turn |
| watch |
| paint |
| like |
| send |
| lend |
| think |

| yellow |
| an invitation |
| the baseball game |
| with anger |
| the author's book |
| one's new hairstyle |
| impolite |

C 그림을 보고 각 보기에서 알맞은 표현을 찾아 윤지가 하루 동안 한 일을 나타내는 문장을 쓰시오.

0  **1**   **2**  **3**

| play a card game   solve the problem   move some furniture |

| tired   excited   embarrassed |

0 *Yunji jogged along the river and she was refreshed.*

1 _____

2 _____

3 _____

UNIT 2 지각동사 / 사역동사 + 목적어 + 목적보어

*Tinker Bell blew the fairy dust and **made Wendy fly**.*
*Wendy **felt her body floating** into the air.*

★ 지각동사와 사역동사의 목적보어로는 보통 동사원형을 쓴다. 하지만, 진행의 의미를 강조할 때는 목적보어로 현재분사를, 목적어와 목적보어가 수동의 관계일 때는 과거분사를 쓴다.

1 지각동사: see, watch, hear, feel, smell
Maria **felt something touch** her feet.
They **saw a man running** toward them.
I **heard my name called**.

2 사역동사: make, let, have
Andrew always **made us laugh** in class.
She **had her car washed** this morning.

> **Note**
> 사역동사의 목적보어로
> 현재분사는 잘 쓰지 않는다.

A 괄호 안의 단어를 배열하여 올바른 문장으로 다시 쓰시오.

1 나는 John이 은행으로 들어가고 있는 것을 보았다. (saw, I, entering, John, the bank)

_____

2 그녀는 미용실에서 머리를 파마했다. (she, her hair, permed, had, at a hair salon)

_____

3 선생님은 우리가 교실을 청소하도록 했다. (made, clean, us, our teacher, the classroom)

_____

4 그녀는 모든 사람이 자신을 보고 있는 것을 느꼈다. (she, everyone, looking at, felt, her)

_____

5 Julia는 어제 그녀의 컴퓨터가 수리되도록 했다.
(her computer, yesterday, Julia, had, repaired)

_____

6 몇몇 사람들이 길 건너에서 총이 발사되는 소리를 들었다.
(heard, fired, across the street, some people, a gun)

_____

7 나의 부모님은 나 혼자 여행하는 것을 허락하지 않는다.
(don't, me, my parents, travel alone, let)

_____

B 보기에서 알맞은 표현을 찾아 우리말에 맞게 영어로 쓰시오.

1 Christine은 어제 그녀의 가방을 도둑맞았다.

   ....

2 그의 아버지는 항상 그가 바닥을 쓸도록 만든다.

   ....

3 아무도 그녀가 방에서 나가고 있는 것을 보지 않았다.

   ....

4 그녀는 라디오에서 그 음악이 연주되는 것을 들었다.

   ....

5 그들은 그 집이 심하게 흔들리고 있는 것을 느꼈다.

   ....

6 나는 나의 어머니가 베이컨을 요리하고 있는 것을 보았다.

   ....

7 Mr. Jones는 그녀가 콘서트에 가는 것을 허락할 것이다.

   ....

> cook bacon
> sweep the floor
> steal
> go to the concert
> play on the radio
> leave the room
> shake badly

C 괄호 안의 표현을 활용하여, 그림을 묘사하는 문장을 쓰시오.

0   (see, fall down / have, go)

   A girl saw a boy falling down.

   She had him go to the hospital.

1   (hear, cry / let, play with)

   1) ....

   2) ....

2  (smell, burn / have, open)

   1) ....

   2) ....

WRAP UP

A 주어진 표현을 활용하여 스트레스를 푸는 방법에 대해 쓰시오.

0
- eat ice cream
- feel good

I usually *eat ice cream* when I'm stressed.

It makes me *feel good.*

1
- go swimming
- feel refreshed

1) _____

2) _____

2
- read comic books
- forget one's problems

1) _____

2) _____

B 그림을 보고 각 보기에서 알맞은 표현을 찾아 그림 속 인물들의 행동을 묘사하시오.

| give |
| look at |
| sweep |
| eat |

| candy |
| the ground |
| ice cream |
| the theme park map |

0   A girl is pointing at the roller coaster.

1   An old man _____ .

2   Two students _____ .

3   A man in a bear costume _____ .

4   A woman with a boy _____ .

C 다음 우리말에 맞게 영어로 쓰시오.

1

Jason은 유명한 영화 감독이 되었다. (movie director)

2

나는 지난주 수요일에 George에게 20달러를 빌려 주었다.

3

그녀의 미소는 항상 나를 행복하게 만든다.

4

그녀는 매일 아침 커피 한 잔을 마신다. (a cup of coffee)

5

그들은 시험 점수가 발표되는 것을 들었다. (announce)

6

나의 아버지는 그 낡은 자동차가 수리되도록 했다.

7

나는 Emma가 내 친구에게 속삭이고 있는 것을 보았다. (whisper to)

D 다음 우리말에 맞게 영어로 쓰시오.

1

1) 나는 어제 Josh가 그의 개와 함께 산책하고 있는 것을 보았다. They looked like they were having fun! When I got home, I asked my mom to buy me a dog. 2) 그러나 그녀는 내가 개를 갖는 것을 허락하지 않았다.

1) ....

2) ....

2

How about coming to the Flower Festival? 1) 당신은 당신의 가족과 함께 아름다운 꽃들을 즐길 수 있습니다. Also, there are lots of fun events. 2) 당신은 우리 웹 사이트로부터 더 많은 정보를 얻을 수 있습니다. Please visit www.FlowerFestival.com.

1) ....

2) .... (from one's website)

E Max의 방에서 손목시계가 사라졌다. 괄호 안의 표현을 활용하여 도난 사건 목격자들의 진술을 쓰시오.

Witness Statement

0   Name: Max (read / hear, walk)
I was reading a book in my room.
I heard someone walking near the window.

1   Name: Amelia (cook / feel, pass by)
1) _____
2) _____

2   Name: Jayden (watch / see, play with)
1) _____
2) _____

F 방학 계획을 세우는 친구에게 무엇을 할지 조언하려고 한다. 다음 제시된 그림을 보고, 주어진 어구를 활용하여 조언하는 메시지를 쓰시오.

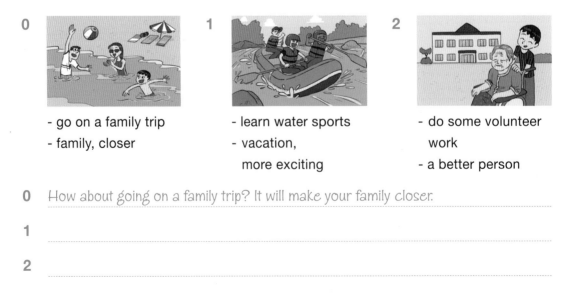

0   - go on a family trip
     - family, closer

1   - learn water sports
     - vacation,
        more exciting

2   - do some volunteer
        work
     - a better person

0   How about going on a family trip? It will make your family closer.

1   _____

2   _____

LESSON 2

문장의 확장 I (접속사)

wake up	boring	earring	stretch
practice	fall asleep	cheerful	go camping
have a cold	catch up with	take part in	toothache
remind	festival	palm	terrible
already	rice	display	burn
full	stew	turn off	tongue
take a shower	contact	flash	hole
ring	mentor	take a picture	go on a picnic
trust	refund	treat	broken
lift	necklace	with care	sneakers

UNIT1 종속접속사로 문장 길게 쓰기 Ⅰ

*Wendy, **when** I count to three, we will be flying!*
If you are scared, close your eyes.

★ 종속접속사를 이용하여 시간, 이유, 조건, 양보의 의미를 나타낼 수 있다.
When I was three, my brother was born.
We jumped into the sea **because** the weather was so hot.
If you see Mr. Simpson, please say hello to him.
Though Sam is short, he can jump high.

Note
자주 쓰는 종속접속사
• 시간: when(~할 때), as(~할 때, ~함에 따라), while(~하는 동안), after(~한 후에), before(~하기 전에)
• 이유: because(~이기 때문에)
• 조건: if(만일 ~라면), unless(만일 ~아니라면)
• 양보: though/although(비록 ~이지만)

A 다음 두 문장을 괄호 안의 단어를 이용하여 한 문장으로 쓰시오.

0 Amanda got home. She called me. (when)

   When Amanda got home, she called me.

1 I got up. My mother woke me up. (before)

   _____

2 You want to be a singer. Practice hard. (if)

   _____

3 Ben has a cold. He eats chicken soup. (when)

   _____

4 They took a taxi. They were very tired. (because)

   _____

5 It rained hard. The boys played soccer. (though)

   _____

6 My father easily forgets things. I remind him. (unless)

   _____

7 Maria ate all the potato chips. She was already full. (though)

   _____

8 My teacher was angry. I didn't do my homework. (because)

   _____

Tips for Writing

종속접속사로 시작하는 종속절이 문장의 앞부분에 올 때는 종속절과 주절 사이에 쉼표(,)를 써서 구분해 준다.

보기에서 알맞은 표현을 찾아 우리말에 맞게 영어로 쓰시오.

1 내일 비가 온다면, 우리는 집에 머물 것이다.

_____

2 비록 나는 친구가 많지만, 행복하지 않다.

_____

3 그는 이메일을 확인한 후에 아침을 먹었다.

_____

4 우리가 TV를 보고 있는 동안 Sam이 저녁을 만들었다.

_____

make dinner
rain
check one's email
have many friends

UNIT 2 종속접속사로 문장 길게 쓰기 II

Captain Hook, you are **such a** bad man **that** I will punish you!

1 ⟨so+형용사/부사+that+주어+동사⟩: 매우 ~해서 …하다
It was **so** hot **that** I took a shower.
They talked **so** loudly **that** I couldn't hear my phone ring.

2 ⟨such a(n)+형용사+명사+that+주어+동사⟩: 매우 ~한 …(이)라서 ~하다
Mary is **such an** honest girl **that** her teacher trusts her.
Daniel was **such a** good swimmer **that** I couldn't catch him.

Note
⟨so ~ that …⟩과 ⟨such a(n) ~ that …⟩은 can[can't]와 함께 잘 쓰인다.

A 다음 두 문장을 ⟨so ~ that …⟩ 또는 ⟨such a(n) ~ that …⟩ 구문으로 연결하여 한 문장으로 쓰시오.

0 He was very happy. He couldn't say anything.
He was so happy that he couldn't say anything.

1 The question was very easy. I could answer it.

_____

2 Mason is a very strong boy. He can lift the desk.

_____

3 The class was very boring. She almost fell asleep.

_____

4 Sophia ran very fast. I could not catch up with her.

_____

5 It was a really great movie. I wanted to see it again.

_____

B 그림을 보고 주어진 표현을 활용하여 각 인물을 묘사하는 문장을 쓰시오.

0

- speak, fast
- understand her

1

- be, young
- drive a car

2

- be, rich
- buy anything

0 Sora speaks so fast that I cannot understand her.

1 _____

2 _____

UNIT 3 상관접속사

I like **both** Wendy **and** Tinker Bell. I can't choose only one!

★ 짝을 이뤄 쓰는 상관접속사는 단어와 단어, 구와 구, 절과 절을 연결하여 쓴다.

1 〈both A and B〉: A와 B 둘 다
Both she **and** her sister went to the festival.

2 〈either A or B〉: A 또는 B
He will be in **either** London **or** Paris this summer.

3 〈neither A nor B〉: A도 B도 아닌
David can speak **neither** Japanese **nor** Chinese.

4 〈not only A but also B〉: A뿐만 아니라 B도 (= B as well as A)
I cooked **not only** rice **but also** stew. (= I cooked stew **as well as** rice.)

> **Note**
> 1 〈both A and B〉 뒤에 오는 동사는 복수형으로 쓴다.
> 2 〈either A or B〉, 〈neither A nor B〉, 〈not only A but also B〉, 〈B as well as A〉 뒤에 오는 동사의 형태는 B의 인칭과 수에 일치시킨다.

A 다음을 상관접속사를 이용하여 고쳐 쓰시오.

0 My father likes playing badminton. I like it, too.
Both my father and I like playing badminton.

1 Susie will buy a jacket, or she will buy a coat.

2 Bill doesn't like action movies, and Kate doesn't either.

3 You can contact us by phone, or you can contact us by email.

4 Mr. White is my teacher. He is also a great mentor.

5 Jessie will come to my birthday party. Kevin will come, too.

6 They gave us a full refund, and they also gave us a free gift.

B 그림을 보고 각 보기에서 알맞은 단어를 골라 그림 속 인물들에 대해 쓰시오.

0 **1** **2** **3**

study   eat   wear

math, history   a necklace, earrings   pizza, a hamburger

0 *Bora will visit both Rome and Paris.*

1

2

3

WRAP UP

A 그림을 보고 각 보기에서 알맞은 표현을 찾아 학교 축제에 참가한 학생들의 경험을 나타내는 문장을 쓰시오.

an exciting experience
a funny game
a great dessert

eat it all
can't stop laughing
told my friend about it

0 I heard a rock band playing. It was such a cheerful song that I danced.

1 I ate a piece of cake.

2 I took part in a yes/no game.

3 I had my palm read.

B 주어진 표현과 종속접속사를 활용하여 각 장소에서 지켜야 할 규칙에 대해 쓰시오.

0
Museum
- be looking at the displays
- take pictures

Don't make any noise when you are looking at the displays.

Turn off the flash before you take pictures.

1
Library
- read them
- enter the library

1) Treat the books with care

2) Turn off your cell phone

2
Swimming Pool
- be in the water
- go into the water

1) Wear a swimming cap

2) Stretch

C 다음 우리말에 맞게 영어로 쓰시오.

1

만약 키가 크고 싶다면, 우유를 매일 마셔라.

2

Kelly와 나는 둘 다 캠핑 가는 것을 좋아한다. (go camping)

3

너나 Mike가 선생님을 도와야 한다.

4

이 컴퓨터는 오래되었을 뿐만 아니라 느리다.

5

Emma는 너무 아파서 학교에 갈 수 없다.

6

나는 너무 심한 치통이 있어서 아무것도 먹을 수 없었다. (bad toothache)

7

내가 일어났을 때, 집에 아무도 없었다.

D 다음 우리말에 맞게 영어로 쓰시오.

1

> I went to a new restaurant yesterday. The food was terrible. 1) 스테이크는 너무 딱딱해서 나는 그것을 먹을 수 없었다. 2) 그들은 나에게 너무 뜨거운 수프를 줘서 나는 혀를 데었다. I will never go there again!

1) _____ (hard)

2) _____ (burn one's tongue)

2

> This morning, my father gave me some money. He told me to buy some things I need to play baseball. 1) 나는 야구 모자뿐만 아니라 야구 방망이도 살 것이다. 2) 하지만 나는 야구 글러브나 야구공은 사지 않을 것이다. I already have them.

1) _____

2) _____

E 다음은 Laura의 쇼핑 리스트이다. 괄호 안의 표현을 활용하여 Laura가 각각의 물건을 사려는 이유를 쓰시오.

0	*Umbrella* (rain / have a hole) I will buy a new umbrella. I can use it when it rains. I need it because mine has a hole in it.
1	*Digital Camera* (go on a picnic / be broken) I will buy a new digital camera. 1) _____ 2) _____
2	*Sneakers* (play badminton / be small) I will buy new sneakers. 1) _____ 2) _____

F 다음 그림을 보고 괄호 안의 표현을 활용하여 교실에 있는 학생들의 행동을 묘사하는 문장을 쓰시오.

There are some students in the classroom.

1 Ian _____ . (not only ~ but also ...)

2 Alicia will _____ . (either)

3 Joshua _____ . (both)

LESSON 3
문장의 확장 II (관계사)

clothing	recommend	reserve	disappointed
manner	language	childhood	price tag
novel	be familiar with	solve	be tired of
useful	introduce	explain	a variety of
stripe	respect	attend	offer
exchange	correct	disagree	discounted
look for	fancy	opinion	outlet
cartoon	for the first time	peel	provide
smelly	laugh at	hold	unlimited
loudly	be born	park	gallery

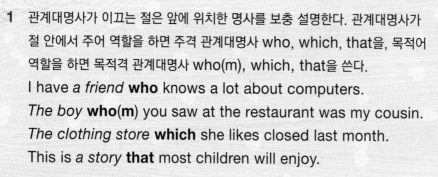

UNIT 1 관계대명사 who(m), which, that, what

Let's follow the golden arrows **which** point to Neverland!
What you see is the beautiful land **that** I live in.

1 관계대명사가 이끄는 절은 앞에 위치한 명사를 보충 설명한다. 관계대명사가 절 안에서 주어 역할을 하면 주격 관계대명사 who, which, that을, 목적어 역할을 하면 목적격 관계대명사 who(m), which, that을 쓴다.

I have *a friend* **who** knows a lot about computers.
The boy **who**(m) you saw at the restaurant was my cousin.
The clothing store **which** she likes closed last month.
This is *a story* **that** most children will enjoy.

2 관계대명사 what은 선행사를 포함하여 the thing(s) that(~하는 것)의 의미로 쓴다.

What made me angry were his bad manners.

> **note**
> 관계대명사로 쓰인 that은 선행사가 사람, 사물인지에 상관없이 쓸 수 있다.

A 다음 문장을 관계대명사를 이용하여 고쳐 쓰시오.

0 I want to read a novel. It is on the best-seller list.

I want to read a novel which[that] is on the best-seller list.

1 The information was useful. I found it on the Internet.

2 I remember the boy. He was wearing a shirt with red stripes.

3 You shouldn't forget the thing that I asked you to do. (what 이용)

4 I want to exchange a pair of shoes. They are too big for me.

5 The boy is at the playground. Mr. and Mrs. Miller are looking for him.

6 This cartoon is the thing that my brother likes most these days. (what 이용)

7 The thing that I want most right now is a glass of water. (what 이용)

B 그림을 보고 보기와 괄호 안의 표현을 활용하여 극장에서 보기 싫은 사람들에 대해 쓰시오.

kick
eat
talk to

1 I don't like people who _____. (smelly food)

2 _____ (other people's seats)

3 _____ (one's friends loudly)

UNIT 2 목적격 관계대명사의 생략

This is a map of Neverland (that) I aways carry.

★ 목적격으로 쓰인 관계대명사는 생략할 수 있다.
She wants to have a sister (**whom**) she can play with.
It is the key (**which**) my father was looking for.
Ricky bought the blue shirt (**that**) his friend recommended.

Note
전치사의 목적어로 쓰인
관계대명사를 생략할 때는
전치사를 관계대명사절의 끝에
쓴다.

A 다음 문장을 생략된 관계대명사를 넣어 다시 쓰시오.

1 Julia will visit the company her father works for.

_____

2 Thomas showed me a photo of a girl he loved.

_____

3 The hotel we stayed at was very close to the airport.

_____

4 The book was written in a language I was not familiar with.

_____

5 I was introduced to the artist I respect the most.

_____

B 그림을 보고 보기에서 알맞은 표현을 골라 어제 여행지에서 겪은 일에 대해 쓰시오.

fancy	eat	take	too old	terrible	buy	expensive	go to

0

The man I met yesterday was kind.

But the map he gave me was not correct.

1

1) The restaurant _____ .

2) But the food _____ .

2

1) The ticket _____ .

2) But the boat _____ .

UNIT 3 관계부사

Do you know **the reason why** Captain Hook is afraid of the crocodile?

★ 관계부사는 시간, 장소, 이유, 방법을 나타내는 절을 이끈다. 선행사가 시간을 나타내는 경우는 when, 장소를 나타내는 경우는 where, 이유나 원인을 나타내는 경우는 why, 방법을 나타내는 경우는 how를 쓴다.
She remembers _the time_ **when** she lived in San Diego.
This is _the park_ **where** we met for the first time.
I don't know _the reason_ **why** she is leaving me.
Aaron wanted to know **how** we got his phone number.

Note

1 관계부사별 흔히 쓰이는 선행사
when: time, day, year 등
where: place, country 등
why: reason 등
2 관계부사 how와 선행사 the way는 함께 쓰지 않고 둘 중 하나만 쓰도록 유의한다.

A 다음 두 문장을 관계부사를 이용하여 한 문장으로 쓰시오.

0 She didn't know the way. He solved the problem in that way.

She didn't know how[the way] he solved the problem.

1 I can't understand why. They laughed at me for that reason.

2 October is the month. I was born in that month.

3 Alex asked me why. I left without a word for that reason.

4 Can you tell me the way? You reserved a seat in that way.

5 He will go to the city. He spent his childhood in that city.

B 보기에서 알맞은 표현을 찾아 우리말에 맞게 영어로 쓰시오.

1 내가 가장 좋아하는 텔레비전 쇼가 시작하는 시간이다.

2 아무도 그녀가 어떻게 부자가 되었는지 모른다.

3 London은 나의 어머니가 태어난 도시이다.

4 네가 그 퍼즐을 어떻게 풀었는지 나에게 말해 줘.

5 그녀는 그녀가 모임에 참석하지 못한 이유를 설명했다.

6 나의 삼촌은 나에게 그가 책을 읽는 방을 보여 주었다.

7 Erin은 나에게 내가 그녀의 의견에 동의하지 않은 이유를 물었다.

read
solve
start
be born
become rich
attend
disagree with

WRAP UP

A 그림을 보고 괄호 안의 표현을 활용하여 Kevin이 동물원에서 본 것에 대한 문장을 쓰시오.

0 I saw a girl who was drawing pictures. (girl, draw)

1 .... (monkey, peel)

2 .... (man, take pictures of)

3 .... (koala, climb)

B 다음 일정표를 보고 Lily의 오늘 일정에 대한 문장을 쓰시오. (주어진 표현을 주어로 사용할 것)

11:00 a.m.	meet Noah
12:30 p.m.	make chicken curry
02:30 p.m.	see the musical *Cats*
06:00 p.m.	go to a party at Jason's house

0 Lily will meet her friend at 11:00 a.m. Noah is the friend whom she is going to meet.

1 Lily will make her lunch at 12:30 p.m.

.... (chicken curry)

2 Lily will see a musical at 2:30 p.m.

.... (*Cats*)

3 Lily will go to a party at 6:00 p.m.

.... (Jason's house)

C 다음 우리말에 맞게 영어로 쓰시오.

1

Amelia는 맛있어 보이는 파이를 골랐다.

2

나는 내 친구가 나에게 사준 그 갈색 모자를 썼다.

3

내게 지금 가장 필요한 것은 휴가이다. (a vacation)

4

그 영화는 배우가 되기를 원하는 한 소년에 관한 이야기이다. (be about)

5

Robert는 그녀가 왜 그에게 화가 나 있는지 모른다.

6

나의 아버지는 그의 차를 주차할 수 있는 장소를 찾고 있다.

7

우리는 그가 너에게 말한 것을 믿을 수가 없다.

D 다음 우리말에 맞게 영어로 쓰시오.

1

> I bought a red skirt from your online shop. 1) 하지만 당신이 나에게 보내 준 것은 무언가 다른 것이에요. It is brown, not red. Plus, it is too big for me. I want to exchange it. 2) 나에게 한 치수 작은 빨간색 치마를 보내 주세요.

1) _____

2) _____ (one size smaller)

2

> There was a big sale yesterday. 1) 세일이 진행 중인 백화점은 나의 집 근처에 있었다. So I went there with my sister. 2) 나는 내가 항상 갖고 싶어하던 선글라스를 사려고 했다. But I was disappointed to see the price tag. It was so expensive even if it was 30 percent off!

1) _____ (go on)

2) _____

E 괄호 안의 표현을 활용하여 광고문을 쓰시오.

0
> *Big Toys* (have a variety of toys / find any toy you can imagine)
>
> Are you tired of the same old toys?
>
> Come to a store which has a variety of toys.
> Big Toys is the place where you can find any toy you can imagine!

1
> *Orange Outlet* (offer discounted clothing / save money)
>
> Do you want to buy new clothes?
>
> 1) Come to a store _____ .
>
> 2) _____

2
> *Top Kitchen* (provide unlimited food / eat as much as you want)
>
> Are you always hungry?
>
> 1) Come to a restaurant _____ .
>
> 2) _____

F 다음 Rodney가 미술 동아리 가입서에 기입한 항목을 보고, 자신을 소개하는 글을 쓰시오.

- Name: *Rodney*
- Something you love to do: *going to art galleries*
- Something you can do well: *drawing cartoons*
- Something you can't do well: *watercolor painting*
- Something you want to learn: *oil painting*

Hi, I'm Rodney.

0 What I love to do is going to art galleries.

1 _____

2 _____

3 _____

Let's be friends!

LESSON 4

문장의 확장 Ⅲ

enough	empty	place	museum
matter	interview	ashamed	camel
wonder	wait in line	lose	desert
earth	pour	liar	fashionable
certain	display	contest	confident
tell a lie	rumor	twist	impression
married	turn out	ankle	play a role
important	false	participate in	gain
strange	surround	decorate	popularity
hurt	receive	work of art	appearance

UNIT 1 명사절을 이끄는 that, whether, if

*I think **that** becoming an adult is terrible!*

1 접속사 that은 '~(이)라는 것'의 의미로 문장에서 주어, 목적어, 보어 역할을 하거나 동격으로 쓰이는 명사절을 이끈다.

It is surprising **that** Jim didn't do his homework.
I think **that** Ms. Reed is a great teacher.
The problem is **that** we don't have enough money.
The fact **that** you are younger than me doesn't matter.

2 whether와 if는 '~인지 아닌지'의 의미로 불확실한 사실을 말할 때 쓴다.
I wonder **whether[if]** Bill will come to the meeting (or not).

> **Note**
> 1 that절이 주어로 쓰일 때는 가주어 it을 사용해서 〈It ~ that〉 구문으로 쓰는 것이 더 자연스럽다.
> 2 that절이 목적어로 쓰일 때는 that을 생략하는 경우가 많다.

A 괄호 안의 단어를 배열하여 올바른 문장으로 다시 쓰시오.

1 나는 Jamie가 나를 정말로 좋아하는지 궁금하다. (likes, wonder, if, I, me, Jamie, really)

....

2 그가 학교에서 인기가 많다는 것은 사실이다. (popular, that, it, he, true, is, at school, is)

....

3 나는 그가 살아 있는지 아닌지 모른다. (or, not, is, don't, whether, know, I, he, alive)

....

4 Mike는 그의 남동생이 정직하다고 믿는다. (that, Mike, honest, is, believes, his brother)

....

5 우리의 계획은 내일 떠나는 것이다. (leave, our, that, plan, tomorrow, we, is, will)

....

6 모든 사람이 지구가 둥글다는 것을 안다. (is, that, knows, round, everybody, the earth)

....

7 나는 재킷을 입어야 하는지 궁금하다. (should, if, I, a jacket, wonder, wear, I)

....

8 Tom이 우리와 함께할지는 확실하지 않다.
(not, certain, us, whether, it, Tom, is, will, join)

....

B 보기에서 알맞은 표현을 찾아 우리말에 맞게 영어로 쓰시오.

1 Sam이 그 지갑을 훔쳤다는 것은 사실이 아니다.

_____

2 나의 어머니는 내가 거짓말을 하고 있다는 것을 알았다.

_____

3 그는 Lisa가 결혼을 했는지 안 했는지 모른다.

_____

4 네가 Kate를 좋아하지 않는다는 사실은 중요하지 않다.

_____

5 Amanda가 일등상을 탄 것은 놀랍지 않다.

_____

6 나는 David가 공부를 하고 있는지 아닌지 모른다.

_____

7 나는 그 뮤지컬이 지금 공연을 하고 있는지 확인할 것이다.

_____

> like
> play
> study
> tell a lie
> be married
> win first prize
> steal the wallet

C 그림을 보고 주어진 표현을 활용하여 각 상황을 나타내는 문장을 쓰시오.

0

- strange, ring
- batteries die

It is strange that my cell phone doesn't ring.

I'm sure that its batteries died.

1

- true, run
- hurt one's leg

1) _____

2) _____

2

- surprising,
  lift the boxes
- be empty

1) _____

2) _____

UNIT 2 형용사구로 문장 길게 쓰기

My friend Tinker Bell is a fairy living in Neverland.

★ 〈분사+전치사구〉 형태의 형용사구는 수식하고자 하는 명사 뒤에서 그 의미를 더욱 구체화한다.

The baby **sleeping in the bed** looks happy.
He interviewed a man **waiting in line** at the station.
The girl **introduced before class** is a new student.
The water **poured from the bottle** is in the bowl.

> **note**
> 명사 뒤의 분사가 현재분사일 때는 능동이나 진행의 의미를, 과거분사일 때는 수동이나 완료의 의미를 나타낸다.

A 괄호 안의 표현을 활용하여 형용사구가 들어간 문장으로 고쳐 쓰시오.

0 The people looked tired. (wait for a bus)

The people waiting for a bus looked tired.

1 My father bought me a new desk. (make of wood)

2 Allison bought the dress. (display in the window)

3 The children are my cousins. (play in the playground)

4 The helicopter is making a loud noise. (fly over the lake)

5 The rumor turned out to be false. (go around the classroom)

6 I know the tall, handsome man. (stand next to the door)

7 The United Kingdom is a European country. (surround by water)

8 The teacher teaches us science. (dress in blue)

> *Tips for Writing*
>
> 주어를 뒤에서 수식하는 어구가 있을 경우에는 특히 동사의 형태가 주어의 수에 일치하는지에 유의한다.

36

각 보기에서 알맞은 표현을 찾아 우리말에 맞게 영어로 쓰시오.

1 나는 프랑스에서 만들어진 핸드크림을 샀다.

2 나는 영어로 쓰인 이메일을 받았다.

3 벤치에 앉아 있는 개는 Tom의 애완동물이다.

4 그 나무 가까이에 서 있는 쌍둥이는 귀엽다.

5 길을 따라 심어져 있는 나무들은 키가 크다.

6 병원에서 나오고 있는 의사는 나의 아버지이다.

7 그 나라에는 물 위에 지어진 집이 많다.

sit
write
make
come
build
stand
plant

in English
in France
near the tree
on the bench
over the water
along the street
out of the hospital

C **그림을 보고 괄호 안의 단어를 활용하여 Steve네 집 거실 풍경을 묘사하시오.**

0 *The vase placed on the table is blue.*   (place)

1 _____ yellow. (stand)

2 _____ Steve. (sit)

3 _____ Steve's dog. (lie)

WRAP UP

A   주어진 표현을 활용하여 각 친구들의 고민에 대해 쓰시오.

0

- not, have many friends, sad
- make friends

The fact that I don't have many friends makes me sad.

But I am not sure whether I can make friends.

1

- not, read many books, ashamed
- make time to read

1)

2)

2

- be always late for school, nervous
- get up early

1)

2)

B   그림을 보고 보기에서 알맞은 표현을 찾아 그림 속 인물들의 행동을 묘사하시오.

stand by   sit on   talk to each other

0   The boy wearing a cap is listening to music.

1   The girl _____ .

2   The man _____ .

3   The children _____ .

C 다음 우리말에 맞게 영어로 쓰시오.

1

마당에 지어진 그 수영장은 크다. (in the yard)

2

주방에서 요리하고 있는 그 소년은 Jacob이다.

3

Sophia는 한국어로 쓰인 책을 읽고 있다.

4

나는 Ella가 집에 있는지 없는지 궁금하다.

5

나는 우리가 종이컵을 사용하지 말아야 한다는 것에 동의한다. (paper cups)

6

그 선수가 그 경기에 졌다는 것은 놀랍다. (lose the game)

7

나는 Tracy가 거짓말쟁이인지 아닌지 모른다.

D 다음 우리말에 맞게 영어로 쓰시오.

1

> 1) Sean이 그 춤 대회에서 우승하다니 놀랍다. He twisted his ankle last week. So he couldn't move well. 2) 나는 그가 대회에 참석할 수 없을 것이라 생각했다. Anyway, I'm proud of him.

1) _____

2) _____ (participate in)

2

> Today is my daughter's birthday. So we planned a party for her. 1) 딸기로 장식된 케이크는 그녀를 위한 내 선물이다. My husband bought a smartphone as a present. 2) 나는 그녀가 우리의 선물들을 좋아할지 궁금하다.

1) _____ (decorate with)

2) _____

E 괄호 안의 표현을 활용하여 여행지에 대한 일기를 쓰시오.

1

(stand in line / display in the museum)

May 2nd

Today I went to the Louvre in Paris, France. 1) There were many people _____ .

2) After an hour of waiting, I enjoyed many works of art _____ . They were beautiful.

2

(some camels, walk across the desert / enter a large pyramid, build with stones)

August 5th

Today I went to the Great Pyramid of Giza in Cairo, Egypt. 1) _____

2) _____ It was an amazing experience!

F 보기에서 알맞은 표현을 찾아 유행 패션을 따라 하는 것의 장점과 단점을 쓰시오.

| cost too much | give a good impression |
| play a role in gaining popularity | make people all look the same |

Advantages

0 I think that wearing fashionable clothes makes people feel confident.

1 _____

2 _____

Disadvantages

0 I think that following fashion trends makes people care too much about their appearance.

1 _____

2 _____

LESSON 5

문장의 확장 IV

driver's license	interviewer	tour	gather
remember	apply	souvenir	forget
on time	skill	leave for	somewhere
drugstore	grocery store	cavity	after a while
nearby	stay	prevent	refund
be interested in	attach	eyesight	deliver
eat out	hold	maintain	auditorium
wallet	on foot	get over	take part in
free	performance	nail	cafeteria
broadcasting	sculpture	hammer	main entrance

UNIT 1 간접의문문

Captain Hook asked Tinker Bell **where Peter Pan lived.**
He asked her **if she could help him catch Peter Pan.**

★ 의문문이 다른 문장의 일부로 쓰인 경우를 간접의문문이라고 하며, 이때
의문문의 어순에 유의한다.

1 의문사가 있는 경우: ⟨의문사+주어+동사⟩

I don't know. Why did he come home so early today?
→ I don't know **why he came** home so early today.

2 의문사가 없는 경우: ⟨if[whether]+주어+동사⟩

Do you know? Is it going to rain tomorrow?
→ Do you know **if[whether] it is** going to rain tomorrow?

Note
주절의 동사가 think, believe,
guess, suppose 등일 때는
의문사를 맨 앞에 쓴다.
Do you **think**? **Who** will win
the game?
→ **Who** do you **think** will
win the game?

A   문장을 다음과 같이 고쳐 쓰시오.

0   I wonder. Why are you waiting here?

   I wonder why you are waiting here.

1   I am not sure. Who will be my partner?

   ....

2   I wonder. Does he have a driver's license?

   ....

3   I can't remember. When is Alex's birthday?

   ....

4   I'd like to know. Did he finish the project on time?

   ....

5   Do you think? Where are they going to meet?

   ....

6   Please tell me. How can I get to the subway station?

   ....

7   Can you tell me? Do you have any plans for this weekend?

   ....

*Tips
for
Writing*

간접의문문이
평서문의 종속절로
쓰였을 때 문장 끝에
물음표(?)를 쓰지
않도록 주의한다.

B 보기에서 알맞은 표현을 찾아 우리말에 맞게 영어로 쓰시오.

| begin |
| put one's wallet |
| be an actor |
| eat out |
| be interested in |
| for the last time |
| get a free coupon |
| a drugstore nearby |

1 그 영화가 몇 시에 시작하는지 아니?

_____

2 그는 내게 왜 배우가 되고 싶은지 물어보았다.

_____

3 Laura는 근처에 약국이 있는지 모른다.

_____

4 나는 그녀가 재즈에 관심이 있었는지 몰랐다.

_____

5 나의 부모님은 나에게 외식하기를 원하는지 물었다.

_____

6 그 남자는 그의 지갑을 어디에 두었는지 기억하지 못한다.

_____

7 나는 우리가 언제 마지막으로 만났는지 확신하지 못한다.

_____

8 나는 그녀가 어떻게 공짜 쿠폰을 얻을 수 있었는지 궁금하다.

_____

C 다음은 학교 방송반 면접에서 면접관이 질문할 내용을 간략히 적어 놓은 메모이다. 메모를 보고 간접의문문을 이용하여 면접 후기를 쓰시오.

I had an interview to join the broadcasting club. The interviewers asked me many questions. First, they wanted to know why I applied.

Questions for Interview
- reason for applying
- broadcasting experience you have
- skills you have
- your dream

1 Then, they wondered _____ .

2 They also asked me _____ .

3 Last, they wanted to know _____ .

I was too nervous. But it was a good experience.

UNIT 2 여러 개의 부사(구) 쓰기

I fought with Captain Hook on his ship with my short sword yesterday.

1 여러 개의 부사(구)를 쓸 때는 보통 〈장소+방법+시간〉의 순서로 쓴다.
I saw Ryan **at the grocery store yesterday.**
They arrived **at Jeju Island by airplane last night.**

2 장소를 나타내는 부사(구) 또는 시간을 나타내는 부사(구)가 각각 둘 이상일 때는
보통 작은 단위에서 큰 단위의 순서로 쓴다.
We are going to stay **at a hotel in Seattle.**
He asked his mother to wake him up **at 7:00 in the morning.**

A 괄호 안의 단어를 배열하여 올바른 문장으로 다시 쓰시오.

1 나는 매일 도서관에서 두 시간씩 공부한다. (every day, study, I, at the library, for two hours)
---

2 그는 버스에서 Alice와 나 사이에 앉았다. (on the bus, sat down, he, between Alice and me)
---

3 그녀는 테이프로 그 사진을 벽에 붙였다. (attached, with tape, she, the photo, to the wall)
---

4 나는 이번 주말에 친구 집에 있을 것이다. (at my friend's house, be, will, this weekend, I)
---

5 그 상점은 토요일 오후 5시에 문을 닫는다. (at 5:00 p.m., the shop, on Saturdays, closes)
---

6 Sean은 오늘 밤 집에서 파티를 열 것이다. (tonight, hold, will, at his house, Sean, a party)
---

7 그들은 방과 후에 체육관에서 농구를 한다.
(play, after school, basketball, they, in the gym)
---

8 그는 여름 방학에 기차를 타고 해변에 간다.
(goes, by train, during summer vacation, to, the beach, he)

B 보기에서 알맞은 표현을 찾아 우리말에 맞게 영어로 쓰시오.

1 나의 아버지는 매일 걸어서 출근한다.

....

2 그녀는 매일 아침 아기를 따뜻한 물로 씻긴다.

....

3 Bella는 다음 주에 버스를 타고 서울을 떠날 것이다.

....

4 몇몇 사람들이 오후에 해변을 따라 거닐고 있다.

....

5 그는 학교 근처에 있는 도서관에서 책을 한 권 빌렸다.

....

6 Kevin은 그 호텔에 삼 일 동안 머물고 있다.

....

7 나는 어젯밤 아홉 시쯤 그녀가 뛰어가고 있는 것을 보았다.

....

> leave
> with warm water
> at the hotel
> along the beach
> at about 9:00
> from the library
> on foot

C 주어진 정보를 활용하여 세계 축제에 대해 쓰시오.

0
- Scotland, 1947
- watch many performances
- summer

The Edinburgh Festival

The Edinburgh Festival has been held in Scotland since 1947.

People enjoy it by watching many performances in summer.

1
- Germany, 1810
- drink beer
- 16 days

Oktoberfest

1) ....

2) ....

2
- Japan, 1950
- look at ice sculptures
- winter

The Sapporo Snow Festival

1) ....

2) ....

WRAP UP

A 여행 일정을 적어 놓은 메모를 보고 다음과 같이 문장을 쓰시오.

> ### Trip Itinerary
>
> **Day Two**
> 09:00   have breakfast / hotel restaurant
> 10:00   take a tour around the island / by boat
> 13:00   buy some souvenirs / traditional market
> 15:00   leave for the airport / by taxi

0 We will have breakfast at the hotel restaurant at 9:00.

1 _____

2 _____

3 _____

B 다음은 종합 병원 인터넷 게시판이다. 주어진 표현을 활용하여 궁금한 점에 대해 문의하는 문장을 쓰시오.

0	- get cavities - prevent cavities	Q: I want to ask you about cavities. Please tell me why people get cavities. Also, I wonder what I should do to prevent cavities.
1	- have bad eyesight - maintain good eyesight	Q: I want to ask you about eyesight. 1) _____ 2) _____
2	- catch colds - get over a cold	Q: I want to ask you about colds. 1) _____ 2) _____

C 다음 우리말에 맞게 영어로 쓰시오.

1

네가 어디에 가고 싶은지 말해 줘.

2

그 남자는 지금 망치로 못을 치고 있다. (hit the nail, hammer)

3

그녀가 언제 파리로 떠날 것이라고 생각하니?

4

그 소년은 교실 안의 책상 아래에 숨었다.

5

그들은 오후 여섯 시에 학교 앞에서 모였다. (gather)

6

Adam은 그 남자의 이름이 무엇인지 기억하지 못한다.

7

나는 그녀에게 여동생이 있는지 궁금하다.

D 다음 우리말에 맞게 영어로 쓰시오.

1

My mother sometimes forgets things. 1) 나는 오늘 아침에 소파에서 자고 있었다. My mother came over. 2) 그녀는 내가 왜 학교에 가지 않는지 물었다. She forgot it was Sunday!

1) _____

2) _____

2

1) Chris는 어제 마당에서 드라이버로 그의 자전거를 고치고 있었다. Then, from somewhere, his cell phone started to ring. 2) 그는 그의 휴대 전화가 어디에 있는지 몰랐다. But after a while, he found it. It was in his pocket!

1) _____ (screwdriver)

2) _____

E 다음은 은희가 전자 제품 매장을 운영하는 아버지를 대신해 전화를 받고 적어 둔 메모이다. 괄호 안의 표현을 활용하여 메모를 쓰시오.

0
Caller: Mrs. Bates
Message:
She asked me if you could give her a refund.

1
Caller: Tony
Message:
_____
_____ (repair one's TV)

2
Caller: Jessica
Message:
_____
_____ (deliver the product)

3
Caller: Mr. Kang
Message:
_____
_____ (send a catalog)

F 다음 표를 보고 괄호 안의 표현을 활용하여 학교 축제에 친구들을 초대하는 이메일을 쓰시오.

Time	Event	Place
1:00 p.m. ~ 3:00 p.m.	*Alice in Wonderland*	auditorium
3:00 p.m. ~ 4:00 p.m.	hot dog eating contest	cafeteria
4:00 p.m. ~ 4:30 p.m.	darts	main entrance

● ● ●

Hi, everyone!
There will be a school festival this Wednesday! Why don't you come?
You can watch the play *Alice in Wonderland* in the auditorium from 1:00 p.m. to 3:00 p.m.

1 _____ (take part in)

2 _____ (play)

Please come and enjoy the festival together! It will be fun.

Best wishes,
Hana

SECTION 2
GRAMMAR FOR WRITING

LESSON 6

시제

east	second	barber	detergent
usually	medicine	parrot	protect
recommend	author	do yoga	environment
freeze	award	relieve	charge
degree	put on	far away	take a rest
boil	wash the dishes	experiment	volunteer
practice	review	dangerous	trick
through	delicious	make a mistake	local
telescope	vet	work	foreigner
attend	treat	break	comfortable

UNIT 1 현재 vs. 현재진행

Captain Hook **is coming** toward us.
I **don't want** to fight him. Let's fly away!

1 현재시제는 일반적인 사실, 불변의 진리, 반복되는 일이나 습관, 상당 기간 동안 지속되는 일 등을 나타낸다.

A year **has** 12 months.　　　　　　The sun **rises** in the east.

I usually **read** news online.　　　　Steven **works** at a fast-food restaurant.

2 현재진행시제는 〈am[are/is]+v−ing〉의 형태로 말하는 시점에 진행 중인 일을 나타낸다.

I **am reading** news online in my room.　　Steven **is working** hard now.

A　괄호 안의 동사를 현재시제 또는 현재진행시제로 바꾸어 문장을 알맞게 고쳐 쓰시오.

1 Hurry up! Your friends (wait) for you.

Hurry up! _____

2 Don't change the channel. I (watch) the show.

Don't change the channel. _____

3 I recommend Grace for the job. She (speak) French well.

I recommend Grace for the job. _____

4 Mrs. Jones (cook) spaghetti now. She (like) to cook.

_____

5 Evan (enjoy) going camping. He (go) camping five times a year.

_____

6 Water (freeze) at 0 degrees Celsius and (boil) at 100 degrees Celsius.

_____

7 I usually (go) to bed late. But today I am tired, so I (go) to bed now.

_____

8 Tom (live) alone, but this week he (stay) at his parents' house in Philadelphia.

_____

9 It (snow) in Korea now. This is the first time I've seen snow because it (not, snow) in my country.

_____

Tips for Writing

같은 명사가 여러 번 나올 때에는 반복하지 않고 대명사로 바꾸어 쓰는 게 좋다.

B 그림을 보고 주어진 표현을 활용하여 각 인물의 평소 습관과 오늘 하고 있는 행동에 대한 문장을 쓰시오.

	0	1	2
Usually	Sean	Miranda	Charlie
Today			
	- go to school	- eat, for a snack	- play, after school

0 Sean usually goes to school on foot.

　　 But today, he is going to school by bus.

1 1) _____

　　 2) _____

2 1) _____

　　 2) _____

C 주어진 표현을 활용하여 친구들의 관심사에 대해 쓰시오.

0　　　Minjun
- join the school band
- practice the drums

Minjun is interested in joining the school band.

So he is practicing the drums now.

1　　　Kimberly
- study the stars
- look at, through a telescope

1) _____

2) _____

2　　　Alex
- learn to cook
- attend a cooking school

1) _____

2) _____

UNIT 2 과거 vs. 현재완료

*My shadow **ran** away from me.*
*But Wendy **has sewn** it onto my body.*

1 과거시제는 동사의 과거형으로 과거의 특정 시점에 일어난 동작이나 상태를 나타낸다.

I **lost** my diary, but I **found** it later.
John **went** to Paris last week, and he **came** back yesterday.

2 현재완료시제는 〈have[has]+v-ed〉의 형태로 과거에 일어난 일이 현재까지
지속되거나 영향을 미치고 있는 상황을 나타낸다.

I can't find my diary. I **have lost** it.
John **has gone** to Paris. I miss him a lot.

> **Note**
> 현재완료시제는 과거의 한 시점을
> 나타내는 yesterday, ago, last
> 등이나 의문사 when과 함께 쓰지
> 않는다.

A 괄호 안의 동사를 과거시제 또는 현재완료시제로 바꾸어 문장을 알맞게 고쳐 쓰시오.

1 This is my second visit to China. I (be) here before.

This is my second visit to China. _____

2 James can't remember her name. He (forget) it.

James can't remember her name. _____

3 Nicole just (finish) her homework. Now she can play computer games.

_____ Now she can play computer games.

4 I (see) Olivia on Tuesday. I (not, see) her since then.

_____

5 I (buy) a book yesterday. But I (not, read) it yet.

_____

6 My brother (be) sick since last night. So he (take) medicine this morning.

_____

7 You (watch) TV too much yesterday, and you already (watch) it for two hours
today.

_____

8 The author (write) a lot of books since 1990, and he (receive) an award last
year.

_____

B   보기에서 알맞은 표현을 찾아 우리말에 맞게 영어로 쓰시오.

put on   take a Spanish lesson   cut one's finger
arrive in   send an email   lose one's cell phone

1   Andrew는 신발 한 켤레를 샀다. 하지만 그는 아직 그것들을 신지 않았다.

---

2   나는 지난주에 캐나다에 도착했다. 나는 이미 많은 장소들을 방문해 왔다.

---

3   Joseph은 작년부터 런던에 있다. 나는 어제 그에게 이메일을 보냈다.

---

4   Emma는 어젯밤에 손가락을 베었다. 그녀는 그때부터 설거지를 하지 않고 있다.

---

5   나는 어제 스페인어 수업을 들었다. 하지만 나는 아직 그것을 복습하지 않았다.

---

6   Emily는 그녀의 휴대 전화를 잃어버렸다. 그녀는 오늘 새 휴대 전화를 샀다.

C   사진을 보고 괄호 안의 표현을 활용하여 스포츠에 관한 경험에 대해 쓰시오.

0   Have you ever played basketball?

- Jenny: I played last year.   (last year)

- Junho: I have played three times.   (three times)

1   1) _____

- Mike: 2) _____   (two months ago)

- Jason: 3) _____   (never)

2   1) _____

- Jina: 2) _____   (last month)

- Julia: 3) _____   (twice)

WRAP UP

A 그림을 보고 각 보기에서 알맞은 표현을 찾아 그림 속 인물들에 대해 쓰시오.

0	1	2	3
Philip	Katie	Peter	Maggie

0 Philip is a cook. He cooks delicious food every day.

But he is washing the dishes now.

practice
treat
cut

1 Katie is a vet. 1) _____

2) _____

2 Peter is a barber. 1) _____

2) _____

play with
play volleyball
cut a dog's hair

3 Maggie is a swimmer. 1) _____

2) _____

B 주어진 표현을 활용하여 다음 애완동물에 대해 쓰시오.

0

Mina
- cat, nine years old
- get, her father
- be a good friend

Mina has had a cat since she was nine years old.

She got it from her father.

She likes it because it is a good friend.

1

Andrew
- parrot, ten years old
- buy, a pet shop
- can talk

1) _____

2) _____

3) _____

2

Lillian
- hamster, six years old
- get, her friend
- be small and cute

1) _____

2) _____

3) _____

C 다음 우리말에 맞게 영어로 쓰시오.

1

그 뮤지컬은 6시에 시작해서 9시에 끝났다. (begin, end)

2

Tony는 2년 동안 샌프란시스코에 살고 있다. (San Francisco)

3

나의 사촌은 내가 그를 마지막으로 본 이후 키가 더 컸다. (grow taller, since)

4

나는 10년 동안 서울에 살았는데, 지금은 뉴욕에 산다.

5

Sarah는 보통 바지를 입는다. 그런데 오늘 그녀는 치마를 입고 있다.

6

Emily는 스트레스를 완화시키길 원하기 때문에 지금 요가를 하고 있다. (relieve one's stress)

7

나의 학교는 멀어서 나는 그곳에 버스를 타고 간다. (far away)

D 다음 우리말에 맞게 영어로 쓰시오.

1

Jina is a member of a science club. She likes to do experiments after school. Right now, She is in the science room. 1) 그녀는 위험한 실험을 하고 있다.
2) 그녀는 어떤 실수도 하고 싶지 않기 때문에 매우 조심하고 있다.

1) ....

2) .... (careful)

2

1) 나는 4월 이후 내 컴퓨터를 두 번 수리했다. It worked well for a few months.
2) 하지만 그것은 어젯밤에 또 고장이 났다. I guess I should buy a new one this time.

1) .... (since)

2) .... (break)

E 괄호 안의 표현을 활용하여 광고문을 쓰시오.

0

(use detergent and water to wash clothes / need water, protect the environment)

PURE Washing Machine

Until now, I have used detergent and water to wash clothes.
But now I'm using a PURE Washing Machine.
It only needs water, so I can protect the environment!

1

(clean one's house oneself / need to be charged, take a rest)

TOP HOUSE Cleaning Robot

1) _____

2) _____

3) _____

F 현재 하고 있는 봉사 활동에 대해 다음 내용을 포함하여 쓰시오.

- what you do and how long you have done it
- why you began
- how often and where you do it

0 I have been volunteering by doing magic tricks for two years.

I began doing it to make people happy.

I do it once a month at local hospitals.

1 1) _____

(teach Korean to foreigners, three years)

2) _____

(help them feel more comfortable in Korea)

3) _____

(every Saturday, a local library)

LESSON 7

조동사

UNIT 1 had better, used to
UNIT 2 기타 조동사

pay attention to	write down	skip	jewelry
keep a diary	apologize	mud	robbery
suit	accident	discuss	theft
bake	appointment	various	track
truth	expect	accept	escape
fever	annoyed	proposal	wig
medicine	bored	have a sore throat	bald
get lost	get along with	advertisement	pursue
downtown	efficiently	sew	suspect
fail an exam	spill	thread	earthquake

UNIT 1 had better, used to

Tinker Bell used to play in the jewel box.
But she is locked in it now. I had better find the key quickly.

1 〈had better+동사원형〉은 '~하는 게 좋겠다'는 충고의 의미로 쓰이며,
부정형은 〈had better not+동사원형〉이다.
You **had better** go see a doctor.
You **had better** *not* eat too much.

2 〈used to+동사원형〉은 '~하곤 했다, ~이었다'의 의미로 과거의 습관이나
상태를 나타낼 때 쓴다.
There **used to** be a big theater near my house.
I **used to** enjoy skiing, but I don't have time for it now.

> **note**
> used to는 '현재는 그렇지
> 않다'는 뜻을 내포한다.

A 괄호 안의 표현을 활용하여 우리말에 맞게 영어로 쓰시오.

1 너는 행동을 조심하는 게 좋겠다. (watch one's behavior)

----

2 나는 방과 후에 Jessica의 집에서 놀곤 했다. (play at, after school)

----

3 우리는 수업 시간에는 선생님에게 집중하는 게 좋겠다. (pay attention to, during classes)

----

4 나는 아이였을 때 Tom을 좋아하곤 했다. (like, when I was a child)

----

5 너는 밤 늦게 친구들을 방문하지 않는 게 좋겠다. (visit, late at night)

----

6 너는 거짓말을 하지 않는 게 좋겠다. (tell a lie)

----

7 나는 어렸을 때 일기를 쓰곤 했다. (keep a diary, young)

----

8 Lauren은 주말에 그녀의 아버지와 등산을 하곤 했다. (climb mountains, on weekends)

B 보기에서 알맞은 표현을 찾아 우리말에 맞게 영어로 쓰시오.

1 우리는 제 시간에 도착하기 위해 지금 떠나는 게 좋겠다.

   ----

2 내가 어렸을 때 내 방에는 많은 장난감이 있었다.

   ----

3 너는 그 면접에 정장을 입는 게 좋겠다.

   ----

4 Angela는 겨울마다 스노보드를 타러 가곤 했다.

   ----

5 너는 아이스크림을 너무 많이 먹지 않는 게 좋겠다.

   ----

6 그녀는 일요일마다 빵을 굽곤 했다.

   ----

7 나의 할아버지는 마당에서 채소를 키우곤 했다.

   ----

8 우리는 그녀에게 그 사실을 말하지 않는 게 좋겠다.

   ----

many toys
the truth
on time
bake bread
go snowboarding
too much
wear a suit
grow vegetables

C 그림을 보고 보기에서 알맞은 표현을 찾아 주어진 상황에서 엄마가 할 수 있는 충고를 쓰시오.

take	stop play	change

0 It is raining heavily. You had better not go outside.

   ----

1 You have a high fever.

   ----

2 Your clothes are too dirty.

   ----

3 It is very late.

UNIT 2 기타 조동사

Captain Hook must have put something in the cake.
You shouldn't have eaten it!

1 〈must have v-ed〉는 '~했음에 틀림없다'의 의미로 과거 사실에 대한 강한 추측을, 〈may have v-ed〉는 '~했을지도 모른다'의 의미로 과거 사실에 대한 약한 추측을 나타낼 때 쓴다.
She isn't answering my calls. She **must have fallen** asleep already.
Anna is not at home yet. She **may have gotten** lost downtown.

2 〈can't[cannot] have v-ed〉는 '~했을 리가 없다'의 의미로 과거 사실에 대한 강한 의심을 나타낸다.
He studied very hard. He **can't have failed** the exam.

3 〈should have v-ed〉는 '~했어야 했다'의 의미로 과거의 일에 대한 후회나 유감을 나타낸다.
I can't remember the address. I **should have written** it down.

A 괄호 안의 표현을 활용하여 우리말에 맞게 영어로 쓰시오.

1 내 여동생이 내 치마를 입었음에 틀림없다. (wear one's skirt)

2 그녀는 그녀의 실수를 사과했어야 했다. (apologize for, mistake)

3 Gwen이 그 초콜릿 케이크를 먹었을 리가 없다. (eat the chocolate cake)

4 Molly가 그에게 사탕을 좀 줬을지도 모른다. (give, some candy)

5 그들은 그 자동차 사고를 보았음에 틀림없다. (see the car accident)

6 너는 그녀의 충고를 들었어야 했다. (listen to one's advice)

7 그녀는 그 결정에 반대했을지도 모른다. (disagree with the decision)

8 그가 그의 중요한 약속을 잊었을 리가 없다. (forget one's important appointment)

B 보기에서 알맞은 표현을 찾아 우리말에 맞게 영어로 쓰시오.

1 Zoe는 어제 그와 같이 있었을지도 모른다.

   _____

2 그들이 내 배낭을 훔쳤음에 틀림없다.

   _____

3 너는 지난주에 표를 예매했어야 했다.

   _____

4 그가 그 파티에서 나를 봤을 리가 없다.

   _____

5 그녀는 그 슬픈 소식을 들었음에 틀림없다.

   _____

6 Hunter는 어렸을 때 가난했을지도 모른다.

   _____

7 John은 그의 어머니에게 화를 내지 말았어야 했다.

   _____

hear
see
be with
steal
be poor
book
be angry with

C 친구와 문자 메시지를 주고받고 있다. 괄호 안의 표현을 활용하여 문자 메시지를 쓰시오.

0

My mother got angry with me.

Why?

I didn't clean my room.

You should have cleaned it. (clean it)

You're right. She cleaned it herself. She must have been tired. (be tired)

1

Isabel is upset with me.

Why?

I forgot her birthday.

1) _____ (remember it)

You're right. She expected a present.
2) _____ (be disappointed)

2

Jayden is annoyed with me.

Why?

I was late again.

1) _____ (be on time)

You're right. He waited for me for an hour.
2) _____ (be bored)

WRAP UP

A 주어진 표현을 활용하여 나의 어린 시절에 대해 쓰시오.

0

- fight with one's brother
- get along with him better

I used to fight with my brother.

I should have gotten along with him better.

1

- stay home every weekend
- do something fun

1) _____

2) _____

2

- play and sleep too much during vacation
- spend one's time more efficiently

1) _____

2) _____

B 그림을 보고 각 보기에서 알맞은 표현을 활용하여 친구들에 대해 추측하는 문장을 쓰시오.

walk
lose
skip

breakfast
one's eraser
through some mud

0 Mike may have spilt water on his T-shirt.

1 Greg _____ .

2 Katie _____ .

3 Bora _____ .

C 다음 우리말에 맞게 영어로 쓰시오.

1

너는 그 지도를 보는 게 좋겠다.

2

우리는 방과 후에 다양한 주제에 대해 토론하곤 했다. (discuss various topics)

3

Roy는 그 개를 무서워했을지도 모른다.

4

Austin이 그들의 제안을 받아들였을 리가 없다. (accept one's proposal)

5

그녀는 목감기에 걸렸음에 틀림없다. (have a sore throat)

6

너는 그 광고를 믿지 말았어야 했다. (advertisement)

7

너는 사탕을 너무 많이 먹지 않는 게 좋겠다.

D 다음 우리말에 맞게 영어로 쓰시오.

1

> Today, I found a hole in my white shirt. I asked my sister to sew it up because she is good at sewing. 1) 하지만 나는 그녀에게 부탁을 하지 말았어야 했다. She sewed it with red thread! 2) 나는 내일 엄마에게 그것을 고쳐달라고 부탁하는 게 좋겠다.

1) _____

2) _____

2

> 1) Ryan은 신발을 백화점에서 사곤 했다. But last week, he bought a pair of shoes on the Internet. The shoes arrived this morning. But they were too small for him. 2) 그는 사이즈를 주의 깊게 골랐어야 했다.

1) _____ (department store)

2) _____ (carefully)

E 괄호 안의 표현을 활용하여 도난 사건을 보도하는 신문 기사를 완성하시오.

1

Jewelry Shop Robbery

There was a theft at the Tiffany Jewelry Shop today. The thief stole a diamond ring. The police found tire tracks by the store. 1) He or she must have _____ . (escape in a car) The police also found a wig. 2) So he or she may have _____ . (be bald) The police are pursuing the suspect.

2

Bank Robbery

There was a theft at Han Bank today. The thief stole a lot of money. The police found glasses in the bank. 1) _____ _____ (have bad eyesight) The police also found a gray hair.

2) _____ (be old) The police are pursuing the suspect.

F 친구에게 지진 발생 시 대피 요령에 대해 충고하려고 한다. 다음 제시된 그림을 보고, 주어진 어구를 활용하여 충고하는 메시지를 쓰시오.

0	1	2

- take an elevator	- get under the table	- get close to any windows

0 You had better not take an elevator during an earthquake.

1 _____

2 _____

LESSON 8

to부정사

vegetable	holiday	amazed	lose weight
rocking chair	save	match	relieve
next	energy	express	farewell party
update	for a long time	feeling	bring
decide	understand	upset	friendly
invite	attractive	racehorse	responsible
take care of	blind	audience	costly
machine	lucky	direction	regularly
vote	zookeeper	friendship	feed
take a trip	play	stand up	smelly

UNIT 1 명사적 용법의 to부정사

I want **to ask** Wendy **to read** me a book.
But I don't know **where to find** her.

1 명사적 용법의 to부정사는 '~하는 것'의 의미로 주어, 목적어, 보어로 쓸 수 있다.
To eat vegetables is good for you.
I want **to buy** a rocking chair.
My dream is **to open** my own restaurant.

2 〈의문사+to부정사〉는 명사구로 쓰이며 의문사에 따라 의미가 달라진다.
The teacher told us **what to do** next.
They didn't know **who(m) to trust**.
Let me know **when to start** the game.
Please tell me **where to turn** left.
I don't know **how to update** the software.

> **note**
> • what to-v: 무엇을 ~할지
> • who(m) to-v: 누구를 ~할지
> • when to-v: 언제 ~할지
> • where to-v: 어디서 ~할지
> • how to-v: 어떻게 ~할지

A 괄호 안의 단어를 배열하여 올바른 문장으로 다시 쓰시오.

1 그는 내일 무엇을 할지 결정하지 못한다. (tomorrow, decide, to, he, can't, do, what)

----

2 Peter는 열쇠를 어디서 찾을지 몰랐다. (didn't, where, Peter, the key, to, know, find)

----

3 Sarah는 빵과 쿠키를 굽는 것을 좋아한다. (to, Sarah, bake, cookies, and, likes, bread)

----

4 나는 파티에 누구를 초대할지 모르겠다. (whom, to, I, know, don't, to the party, invite)

----

5 나는 아기를 돌보는 것이 어렵다는 것을 알았다.
(babies, found, I, it, take care of, difficult, to)

----

6 재호는 나에게 그 기계를 사용하는 법을 가르쳐 주었다.
(taught, use, me, the machine, to, how, Jaeho)

----

7 Jenny는 나에게 내일 그녀를 언제 만날지 이야기했다.
(told, Jenny, tomorrow, to, me, her, when, meet)

B 보기에서 알맞은 표현을 찾아 우리말에 맞게 영어로 쓰시오.

1 이 상자를 어디에 둘지 내게 말해 줘.

   ----

2 Hailey는 자동차 운전하는 법을 배웠다.

   ----

3 그들은 누구에게 투표할지 결정했다.

   ----

4 Jordan은 저녁 식사로 무엇을 요리할지 몰랐다.

   ----

5 나는 이번 주말에 해변에 가기를 원한다.

   ----

6 운동을 하는 것은 너의 건강에 좋다.

   ----

7 그녀의 계획은 이번 주말에 시험공부를 하는 것이다.

   ----

vote for
cook for dinner
put
exercise
go to the beach
study for the test
drive a car

C 메모를 보고 주어진 표현을 활용하여 휴일에 하고 싶은 일에 대해 쓰시오.

0

Movie
- What movie?
- How do I get to the cinema?

Anna wants to watch a movie this weekend.

But she can't decide what to watch.

And she doesn't know how to get to the cinema.

1

Trip
- Where?
- What should I do first?

Paul wants to take a trip on this holiday.

1) --

2) --

2

Cake
- With whom?
- How do I make it?

Christine wants to make a cake on Christmas.

1) --

2) --

UNIT 2 형용사적·부사적 용법의 to부정사

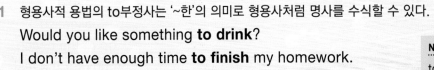

*The crocodile is looking for something **to eat**.*
*Captain Hook is surprised **to see** the crocodile.*

1 형용사적 용법의 to부정사는 '~한'의 의미로 형용사처럼 명사를 수식할 수 있다.
   Would you like something **to drink**?
   I don't have enough time **to finish** my homework.

2 부사적 용법의 to부정사는 '~하기 위해(목적)', '~해서(원인)' 등의 의미로
   부사처럼 동사, 형용사, 부사를 수식할 수 있다.
   Turn off the lights **to save** energy.
   I am sorry **to keep** you waiting for a long time.

> **Note**
> to부정사가 쓰인 주요 구문
> • 〈too ~ to-v〉: 너무 ~해서 …할
>   수 없다
>   I was **too** sleepy **to** watch
>   the movie.
> • 〈enough to-v〉: ~할 수 있을
>   만큼 충분히 …하다
>   She can see well **enough**
>   **to** read the sign.

A 괄호 안의 단어를 배열하여 올바른 문장으로 다시 쓰시오.

1 Ellie는 그녀를 도와줄 누군가가 필요하다. (someone, Ellie, to, her, help, needs)

   _____

2 그는 청바지를 사기 위해 그 가게에 갔다. (went, the store, he, to, to, jeans, buy)

   _____

3 우리는 영화를 보기 위해 영화관에 갔다. (the cinema, to, a movie, we, to, went, watch)

   _____

4 나는 시험에서 좋은 점수를 받아서 기뻤다.
   (on the test, get, to, was, good, glad, I, score, a)

   _____

5 Julia는 너무 어려서 그 책을 이해할 수 없다.
   (the book, to, Julia, understand, too, is, young)

   _____

6 Chris는 그 버스를 잡을 수 있을 만큼 빨리 뛰었다.
   (to, the bus, fast, ran, catch, Chris, enough)

   _____

7 이 도시에는 방문할 매력적인 장소가 많다.
   (many, there, visit, in this city, attractive, to, are, places)

   _____

B 보기에서 알맞은 표현을 찾아 우리말에 맞게 영어로 쓰시오.

1 나는 너에게 이야기할 좋은 소식이 있다.

   ----

2 그들은 앉을 벤치를 찾고 있다.

   ----

3 나의 휴대 전화는 너무 커서 내 주머니에 넣을 수 없다.

   ----

4 나의 부모님은 내가 춤추는 것을 보고 행복해하셨다.

   ----

5 Bill은 돈을 아끼기 위해 걸어서 학교에 갔다.

   ----

6 그녀는 Debbie가 장님인걸 알게 되면 놀랄지도 모른다.

   ----

7 Jim은 홈런 공을 잡을 수 있을 만큼 운이 좋았다.

| lucky |
| sit on |
| on foot |
| good news |
| put in one's pocket |
| be surprised to |
| dance |

C 주어진 표현을 활용하여 친구들이 현재의 꿈을 갖게 된 계기에 대해 쓰시오.

0 Juhui
   - the zoo, the animals
   - happy, a cute baby bear

   I once went to the zoo to see the animals.
   I was very happy to see a cute baby bear.
   After that, I decided to become a zookeeper.

1 Samuel
   - the theater, a play
   - amazed, such a great performance

   1) --
   2) --
   After that, I decided to become an actor.

2 Brooke
   - a tennis court, a tennis match
   - excited, the great match

   1) --
   2) --
   After that, I decided to become a tennis player.

WRAP UP

A 다음 Luis의 여행 계획에 관한 그림을 보고 주어진 대답에 알맞은 질문을 쓰시오.

0 　1　　2　　3

Luis will go abroad this year.

0 ~~Did he decide where to go?~~ – Yes, he will go to Egypt.

1 .... – Yes, he will go there on July 10th.

2 .... – Yes, he will go there by airplane.

3 .... – Yes, he will go there with Evan.

B 보기에서 알맞은 표현을 고른 후, to부정사를 활용하여 기념일에 대한 일기를 쓰시오.

| see the pretty house | see one's friends eat it |
| give to one's parents | express one's feelings |

1

Serena's Diary　　　　　　　　　　　　　　　　　　February 14th

Today was Valentine's Day. 1) I gave Jim some chocolate

....

2) But I was upset ....

I was sad.

2

Hojin's Diary　　　　　　　　　　　　　　　　　　　May 8th

Today was Parents' Day. 1) I bought carnations ....

.... I also decorated the house with

some balloons. 2) My parents were happy ....

.... I was also happy.

C 다음 우리말에 맞게 영어로 쓰시오.

1

그 경주마는 너무 늙어서 경주에서 달릴 수 없다. (racehorse, in the race)

2

나는 관중 앞에서 무엇을 말할지 잊어버렸다. (the audience)

3

나는 길을 물어볼 누군가를 찾고 있다. (ask for directions)

4

그의 계획은 진정한 우정에 대한 영화를 만드는 것이다.

5

Alicia는 그 선물에 대해 그에게 어떻게 감사해야 할지 모른다.

6

그 사람들은 별똥별을 더 잘 보기 위해 일어섰다. (shooting stars)

7

나는 그 야구 경기의 점수를 듣고 놀랐다.

D 다음 우리말에 맞게 영어로 쓰시오.

1

Mark went on a trip to Paris. He took some pictures at the Eiffel Tower. On his way back to the hotel, he got lost. 1) 그는 누구에게 도움을 청할지 몰랐다. Then a woman came up to him. 2) 그녀는 그에게 호텔에 가는 방법을 이야기해 줬다.

1) _____ (ask for help)

2) _____

2

I do yoga every day. 1) 나는 살을 빼고 싶었기 때문에 그것을 하기 시작했다. It really helped me lose weight. And it also relieves my stress. 2) 나는 긴장을 풀 방법을 찾아서 기쁘다.

1) _____

2) _____ (relax)

E 주어진 표현을 활용하여 파티 정보를 묻는 메모를 쓰시오.

0

| - the time of the party |
| - the things to bring to the party |

Do you know anything about Mia's farewell party? I don't know when to go. I don't know what to bring to the party, either. Please call me.

Devin

1

| - the way to get to the party place |
| - the present to buy him |

Do you know anything about Cody's birthday party?

1) ....

2) ....

Please call me.

Isaac

F 주어진 표현을 활용하여 애완동물 기르는 것의 장점과 단점에 대한 문장을 쓰시오.

Advantages	Disadvantages
- friendly, relieve stress	- costly, keep
→ act cute, make you happy	→ buy pet food regularly, feed them
- difficult, make you responsible	- smelly, play with
→ take care of pets, learn to be responsible	→ wash them often, make them smell better

Advantages

0 Pets are friendly enough to relieve stress.

For example, they act cute to make you happy.

1 1) Keeping pets is ....

2) So you can ....

Disadvantages

0 Pets are too costly to keep.

For example, you have to buy pet food regularly to feed them.

1 1) Some pets are ....

2) So you should ....

LESSON 9

비교급과 최상급

previous	novel	athlete	believe
laptop	dish	respected	recycle
climb	storm	generous	throw away
strict	scene	experience	trash
complicated	voice	bright	intelligent
worry	stylish	cheerful	energetic
grade	weight	notice	activity
attention	thickness	focus on	useful
throw	storage	terrible	discussion
far	capacity	downtown	creative

UNIT1 원급, 비교급 표현

*Tinker Bell is getting **weaker and weaker.***
*The **more** children believe in fairies, **the stronger** she becomes.*

1 〈as+원급+as〉: ~만큼 …한
I hope his new album is **as great as** his previous work.

2 〈배수사+as+원급+as〉 = 〈배수사+비교급+than〉: ~의 …배로 ~한
This laptop is **three times as expensive as** that one.
= This laptop is **three times more expensive than** that one.

> **note**
> 배수사 twice의 경우 보통 〈twice +as+원급+as〉의 형태로 쓴다.

3 〈비교급+and+비교급〉: 점점 더 ~한
The days are getting **longer and longer** now.

4 〈the+비교급 ~, the+비교급 …〉: ~할수록, 더 …하다
The higher you climb, **the colder** the air becomes.

A 괄호 안의 단어를 배열하여 올바른 문장으로 다시 쓰시오.

1 Ian은 나보다 두 배 더 많이 먹는다. (much, Ian, me, as, eats, twice, as)

_____

2 그는 요새 점점 더 키가 크고 있다. (these days, taller, getting, taller, and, is, he)

_____

3 나는 더 많이 잘 수록, 더 피곤함을 느낀다. (the more, I, the more, tired, I, feel, sleep)

_____

4 그가 늦게 올수록, 그녀는 더 화가 난다. (the angrier, is, comes, he, she, the later)

_____

5 점점 더 많은 학생들이 스마트폰을 사용하고 있다.
(and, students, using, more, smartphones, are, more)

_____

6 나의 아버지는 내 여동생보다 세 배 더 무겁다.
(is, heavier, my sister, than, my father, three times)

_____

7 Amy는 나만큼 이름을 잘 외울 수 있다.
(as, remember, can, well, names, as, I, Amy, can)

_____

B 보기에서 알맞은 단어를 찾아 우리말에 맞게 영어로 쓰시오.

1 Bailey는 점점 더 아름다워지고 있다.

   ....

2 나의 고양이는 점점 더 살이 찌고 있다.

   ....

3 그 호텔 방은 내 방보다 두 배 더 컸다.

   ....

4 그녀의 부모님은 나의 부모님만큼 엄격하다.

   ....

5 이 문제는 저것보다 열 배 더 복잡하다.

   ....

6 나는 Evan만큼이나 그 시험에 대해 걱정한다.

   ....

7 열심히 공부할수록, 너의 성적은 더 좋아질 것이다.

   ....

8 아이들은 나이가 어릴수록, 더 많은 보살핌이 필요하다.

   ....

| beautiful |
| worried |
| complicated |
| heavy |
| young |
| large |
| good |
| strict |

C 다음 육상 기록을 보고 보기에서 알맞은 단어를 찾아 육상 경기 결과에 대해 쓰시오.

| far   fast   jump   run |

0 **Throwing a ball**
   Mia: 10 m
   Julia: 40 m

   Mia couldn't throw a ball as well as Julia.

   Julia threw a ball four times as far as Mia.

1 **The 100 meters**
   Zoe: 28 sec
   Sophia: 14 sec

   ....

   ....

2 **The long jump**
   Tony: 50 m
   Ryan: 150 m

   ....

   ....

UNIT 2 최상급 표현

I am **one of the most popular boys** in Neverland.
I have many friends. Tinker Bell is **the smallest of** my friends.

1 〈the+최상급+(in[of] ~)〉: ~ 중에서 가장 …한
Russia is **the biggest** country **in** the world.

2 〈one of the+최상급+복수명사〉: 가장 ~한 것들 중 하나
Lionel Messi is **one of the greatest soccer players** ever.

3 〈비교급+than any other+단수명사〉: 다른 어떤 ~보다 더 …하다
His novels are **more interesting than any other book**.

4 〈비교급+than all the other+복수명사〉: 다른 모든 ~보다 더 …하다
This hotel is **cheaper than all the other hotels** in town.

A 괄호 안의 표현을 활용하여 우리말에 맞게 영어로 쓰시오.

1 어제는 내 인생에서 가장 행복한 날이었다. (happy, of my life)

2 John은 그의 반에서 가장 키가 큰 소년이다. (tall, in one's class)

3 그는 우리 반에서 가장 게으른 학생 중 하나이다. (one, lazy, in one's class)

4 이 자동차는 다른 모든 자동차들보다 편안하다. (this car, comfortable)

5 이 요리는 그 식당의 다른 어떤 요리보다 맛있다. (this dish, delicious, in the restaurant)

6 Sarah는 그 병원에서 가장 친절한 간호사 중 하나이다. (one, kind, in the hospital)

7 허리케인은 다른 어떤 종류의 폭풍보다 위험하다. (a hurricane, dangerous, storm)

8 이 장면은 이 영화의 다른 어떤 부분보다 흥미진진하다.
(this scene, exciting, any other part, of this movie)

B 보기에서 알맞은 표현을 찾아 우리말에 맞게 영어로 쓰시오.

1 1월은 1년 중 가장 추운 달이다.
_____

2 Mrs. Wood는 다른 모든 선생님들보다 인기가 있다.
_____

3 이 스웨터는 그 가게의 다른 어떤 스웨터보다 따뜻해 보인다.
_____

4 그는 한국에서 가장 매력적인 배우들 중 하나이다.
_____

5 그녀의 책상은 그 교실에 있는 다른 어떤 책상보다 더 더럽다.
_____

6 Jack Sparrow는 그 영화에서 가장 독특한 캐릭터 중 하나이다.
_____

7 그녀는 우리 반에서 가장 아름다운 목소리를 가졌다.
_____

8 이 슬리퍼는 그 가게에 있는 다른 모든 신발들보다 싸다.
_____

cheap
popular
cold
dirty
warm
attractive
beautiful voice
unique character

C 그림을 보고 괄호 안의 단어를 활용하여 점원이 손님에게 옷에 대해 설명하는 문장을 쓰시오.

0   1   2   3

0   This shirt is cheaper than all the other shirts here.   (cheap)

1   _____ (stylish)

2   _____ (warm)

3   _____ (cute)

WRAP UP

A 다음 표를 보고 괄호 안의 단어를 활용하여 두 카메라를 비교하는 문장을 쓰시오.

Model	DS308	DG487
Screen Size	1.5 inches	1.5 inches
Price	$300	$150
Weight	540 g	180 g
Thickness	2.7 inches	0.9 inches
Storage Capacity	2GB	2GB

0 DS308's screen is as big as DG487's. (big)

1 DS308 _____. (expensive)

2 DS308 _____. (heavy)

3 DS308 _____. (thick)

4 DS308's _____. (big)

B 주어진 표현을 활용하여 닮고 싶은 사람에 대해 쓰시오.

0
- famous, athlete
- fast, person

I want to be like Usain Bolt.

He is one of the most famous athletes in the world.

I think he is faster than any other person.

1
- respected, woman
- generous, person

I want to be like Mother Teresa.

1) _____

2) _____

2
- popular, movie star
- handsome, actor

I want to be like Johnny Depp.

1) _____

2) _____

C 다음 우리말에 맞게 영어로 쓰시오.

1

_____

빗소리가 점점 커지고 있다. (the sound of, loud)

2

_____

네가 더 많은 장소를 여행할수록, 너는 더 많은 경험을 할 것이다. (experience, have)

3

_____

양쯔 강은 중국에 있는 다른 어떤 강보다 길다. (the Yangtze River)

4

_____

시리우스는 밤하늘에서 가장 밝은 별이다. (Sirius)

5

_____

Blake는 그 마을의 다른 모든 소년들보다 쾌활하다. (cheerful)

6

_____

이번 달에, 나는 지난달보다 두 배만큼 많은 돈을 썼다.

7

_____

그는 미국에서 가장 재미있는 코미디언들 중 하나이다. (funny, comedian)

D 다음 우리말에 맞게 영어로 쓰시오.

1

> 1) Kimberly는 우리 반의 다른 어떤 소녀보다 예뻐. Today I was invited to her house. As I entered her room, I noticed a hole in my sock. 2) 그 구멍은 점점 커지고 있는 것 같았어. I couldn't focus on what she was saying. It was terrible!

1) _____ (pretty)

2) _____ (seem to)

2

> I bought a flower-print bag downtown. 1) 그것은 요즘 가장 유행하는 가방들 중의 하나이다. I carried it every day. But yesterday I found the same bag on the Internet. 2) 그것은 내것보다 세 배가 쌌다. I can't believe it!

1) _____ (fashionable)

2) _____

E 괄호 안의 단어를 활용하여 캠페인 문구를 쓰시오.

0

> ***Recycle to Help the Earth!*** (throw away, much trash / recycle, healthy)
>
> People are throwing away more and more trash.
> So why don't you recycle to help the Earth?
> The more you recycle, the healthier the Earth can be!

1

> ***Read to Become Smarter!*** (read, little / read, intelligent)
>
> 1) _____
>
> So why don't you read to become smarter?
>
> 2) _____

F 동아리에 가입하려고 하는 후배에게 동아리를 추천하려고 한다. 다음 제시된 그림을 보고, 주어진 어구를 활용하여 추천하는 메시지를 쓰시오.

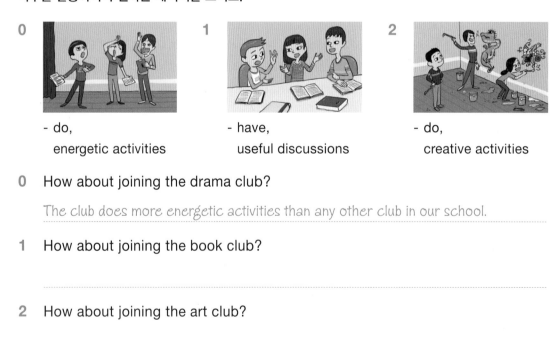

0
- do,
  energetic activities

1
- have,
  useful discussions

2
- do,
  creative activities

0 How about joining the drama club?

The club does more energetic activities than any other club in our school.

1 How about joining the book club?

_____

2 How about joining the art club?

_____

LESSON 10

기타

own	underwear	book	take part in
so far	exercise	opportunity	talent
yet	health	pose	permission
during	the elderly	require	choose
transfer	station	rotten	carefully
price	wedding	hole	character
avoid	joke	because of	touching
waste	library	lyric	faith
electricity	agree with	experiment	peel
turn off	increase	firefighter	in detail

UNIT 1 동사 have의 용법

*Wendy **had** a warm heart. So I **had** her take care of the children.*
*Since then, she **has read** a book to them every evening.*

★ 동사 have에는 다음과 같은 여러 가지 쓰임이 있다.

1 일반동사 have는 '가지다, 먹다'의 의미로 쓴다.
My sister wants to **have** her own room.

2 사역동사 have는 〈have+목적어+목적보어(동사원형/과거분사)〉의 형태로 쓰여 '~시키다, ~하게 하다'의 의미로 쓴다.
My mother **has** *me do* the dishes on weekends.

3 조동사 have는 〈have+v-ed〉 형태의 완료형에 쓰여 '(이전부터 죽) ~했다'의 의미로 쓴다.
James **has**n't **eaten** anything since yesterday.

A 괄호 안의 표현과 have를 활용하여 우리말에 맞게 영어로 쓰시오.

1 나는 John이 저녁을 요리하도록 시킬 것이다. (cook, dinner)

----

2 나는 지금까지 5개의 시험을 봤다. (take, exam, so far)

----

3 나는 아직 내 방을 청소하지 않았다. (clean, my room, yet)

----

4 Dylan은 그 벽이 파란색으로 페인트칠되도록 했다. (the wall, paint)

----

5 나의 엄마는 오늘 아침에 커피 한 잔을 마셨다. (a cup of coffee)

----

6 나의 할아버지는 내가 그에게 책을 읽어 드리도록 했다. (read, a book)

----

7 우리는 여름 방학 동안 싱가포르에서 좋은 시간을 가졌다.
(a nice time, Singapore, summer vacation)

> *Tips for Writing*
>
> 주어가 3인칭 단수인 현재시제 또는 현재완료시제의 문장에서는 have가 아닌 has로 쓰는 것에 유의한다.

B 보기에서 알맞은 표현을 찾아 우리말에 맞게 영어로 쓰시오.

1 나의 아버지는 Kevin이 내 사진을 찍도록 했다.

....

2 우리는 5년 동안 서로 알아 왔다.

....

3 나의 가족은 전에 영국에 가 본 적이 없다.

....

4 나의 선생님은 영어 수업 시간에 내가 그 책을 읽도록 했다.

....

5 Grace는 점심으로 치킨 샌드위치와 오렌지 주스를 먹었다.

....

6 그는 이 학교에 전학 오기 전에 많은 친구들이 있었다.

....

7 너는 인터넷에서 옷을 싼값에 산 적이 있니?

....

> for lunch
> transfer to
> be to England
> read the book
> at a cheap price
> know each other
> take one's picture

C 그림을 보고 괄호 안의 표현을 활용하여 자원 절약에 대해 쓰시오.

0 (water, use a cup)

Our teacher had us avoid wasting water.

Since then, we have used a cup when we brush our teeth.

1 (electricity, turn off the lights)

1) ....

2) .... when we leave a room.

2 (energy, wear long underwear)

1) ....

2) .... in winter.

UNIT 2 특수구문

I do not always fly. Flying every day is hard.
But I always sing and dance!

1 부분부정: 〈not+all[every, always]〉(모두가[항상] ~인 것은 아니다)
Not all the students play computer games like you.

2 수 일치: 동사의 형태를 주어의 수에 일치시킨다.

1) 단수 취급하는 경우: each, every, -thing, -one, -body, 동명사구, 〈the number of+복수명사〉(~의 수) 등
Something **is** wrong.
Exercising every day **is** good for your health.

2) 복수 취급하는 경우: 〈the+형용사〉(~한 사람들), 〈a number of+복수명사〉(많은 ~) 등
The elderly **have** more time to travel.
A number of school events **are** held in spring.

3 병렬 관계: and, but, or 등의 접속사로 연결된 단어나 어구들은 동일한 문법 형태와 구조로 쓴다.
He likes **to travel** *and* **to take** pictures of everything.

> **Note**
> 기타 수 일치
> 〈either A or B〉, 〈neither A nor B〉, 〈not only A but (also) B〉, 〈B as well as A〉는 B의 수에 동사의 형태를 일치시키고, 〈both A and B〉는 동사를 복수형으로 쓴다.

A 괄호 안의 단어를 배열하여 올바른 문장으로 다시 쓰시오.

1 역에 있는 각각의 사람은 피곤해 보인다. (in the station, person, tired, each, looks)

_____

2 모두가 그 결혼식에 오지는 않을 것이다. (the wedding, will, to, everyone, come, not)

_____

3 그의 농담이 언제나 우리를 웃게 하지는 않는다. (not, jokes, laugh, his, always, us, do, make)

_____

4 매일 5마일을 걷는 것은 쉽지 않다. (every day, not, five miles, is, walking, easy)

_____

5 그녀는 교실이 아니라 도서관에 있다. (not, is, in the library, she, but, in the classroom)

_____

6 많은 사람들이 그 경기를 보고 있다. (watching, people, are, the game, a number of)

_____

7 그는 등산과 낚시를 즐긴다. (he, and, climbing, enjoys, fishing, mountains)

_____

B 보기에서 알맞은 표현을 찾아 우리말에 맞게 영어로 쓰시오.

1 우리 모두가 그의 의견에 동의하지는 않는다.

2 우리 학교의 학생 수가 증가하고 있다.

3 Emma는 버스를 타거나 걸어서 학교에 간다.

4 뉴욕행 비행기 표를 예매하는 것은 어려웠다.

5 Joseph이 일요일에 언제나 교회에 가는 것은 아니다.

6 각각의 학생들은 그 프로그램에 참여할 기회가 있다.

7 Mike는 TV 보는 것과 축구 하는 것을 좋아한다.

> book
> all of us
> go to church
> attend the program
> increase
> on foot
> like

C 그림을 보고 보기에서 알맞은 표현을 찾아 소풍을 온 학생들의 모습을 묘사하시오.

> fun
> wear a school uniform
> enjoy it
> dance to music
> wear one
> be required

0 Posing in front of a camera is exciting. But not all the students like it.

1 1)

   2)

2 1)

   2)

WRAP UP

A   그림을 보고 주어진 표현을 활용하여 친구를 소개하는 문장을 쓰시오.

0	1	2	3
- read, 100 books	- make, 10 cakes	- write, 15 novels	- see, 12 plays

0   I have a friend who likes to read books. He has read 100 books so far.

1

2

3

B   그림을 보고 주어진 표현을 활용하여 마트에서 구입한 물건에 대해 쓰시오.

0   - all, red
      - a number of, rotten

I bought a box of apples.

But not all the apples are red.

And a number of the apples are rotten.

1   - every, soft
      - each, dirty

I bought five towels.

1)

2)

2   - all, big
      - every, have a hole in it

I bought three umbrellas.

1)

2)

C 다음 우리말에 맞게 영어로 쓰시오.

1

John은 많은 책을 갖고 있지만, 그것들을 읽지 않는다.

2

그 가수는 전 세계의 많은 도시에서 콘서트를 해 왔다.

3

나는 그것의 멜로디 때문이 아니라 그것의 가사 때문에 그 노래를 좋아한다. (melody, lyrics)

4

숲 속을 걷는 것은 내가 기분 좋게 느끼도록 만든다. (woods)

5

매년 많은 쥐들이 실험에 사용된다. (a number of, in experiments)

6

그 소방관은 그 아이들이 그들의 코와 입을 젖은 수건으로 가리도록 했다. (cover, with)

7

모든 학생이 그 장기 자랑에 참여하길 원하는 것은 아니다. (take part in, talent show)

D 다음 우리말에 맞게 영어로 쓰시오.

1

> 1) 나는 작년부터 이 집에 살아왔다. It is old, but I really like it. 2) 그것은 내가 강을 볼 수 있는 아름다운 발코니를 갖고 있다. I like to spend time sitting there and reading a book.

1) ....

2) .... (where)

2

> Many students want to have a dog. 1) 그러나 개를 돌보는 것은 쉽지 않다. 2) 당신은 그것을 먹이고, 산책시키고, 씻겨야 한다. You also need your family's permission. 3) 그러나 모두가 개들을 좋아하는 것은 아니다. So you should choose carefully.

1) .... (taking care of)

2) .... (feed)

3) .... (everyone)

E 괄호 안의 표현을 활용하여 책을 추천하는 글을 쓰시오.

0

I read a comic book called *The Boxer*.

The action scenes are very exciting.

I like the book a lot, so I have read it three times. (three times)

Read this book and have a great time! (a great time)

1

I read a fantasy novel called *The Dragons*.

The characters are very interesting.

1) .... (twice)

2) .... (an exciting experience)

2

I read a book called *Fly High*.

The story is very touching.

1) .... (four times)

2) .... (faith in your dreams)

F 주어진 정보와 괄호 안의 단어를 활용하여 Peel the Shrimp 대회를 소개하는 이메일을 쓰시오.

- Date: October 23ʳᵈ
- How to win: peel and eat two shrimp
- Age limit: 16 or older
- Do not: use two hands

● ● ●

This year's "Peel the Shrimp" contest will be held on October 23ʳᵈ.
I'll explain the contest in detail.

1 First, ... enter the contest. (everyone)
You must be 16 or older.

2 Second, ... to win. (must)
The fastest person will be the winner.

3 Third, ... not permitted. (be)
If you are 16 or older, please come and join us!

LESSON 11
가정법

headache	broom	work for	attend
marathon	explore	be jealous of	earplug
route	the North Pole	shop for groceries	concentrate on
confused	polar bear	take care of	text message
spend time with	igloo	jump rope	for a while
sleepy	perfect score	relax	past
receive	afford to	be short of	ancient
present	opportunity	do volunteer work	age
appear	opinion	break one's promise	dinosaur
wizard	suspect	professional	dynasty

UNIT 1 가정법 과거

If I lived in the real world, I would grow older.

★ 〈If+주어+동사의 과거형 ~, 주어+would[could, might]+동사원형 ...〉의
가정법 과거는 '~(이)라면 ···할 텐데'의 의미로 현재 사실과 반대되거나 실현
가능성이 거의 없는 일을 가정할 때 쓴다.
If I **were** an adult, I **would** not **have** to take tests.
If he **had** time, he **could take** you home.
If there **were** no homework, I **would be** very happy.

> **Note**
> 가정법 과거에서 if절에 쓰는
> be동사는 주어의 인칭과 수에
> 관계없이 were를 쓴다.

A 문장을 다음과 같이 고쳐 쓰시오.

0 Julia lives far away, so I can't see her often.

If Julia didn't live far away, I could see her often.

1 It is snowing heavily, so we can't climb the mountain.

- -

2 I have a headache, so I can't run in the marathon.

- -

3 He doesn't save money, so he can't buy a new headset.

- -

4 That store isn't open on Sundays, so I have to find another one.

- -

5 She doesn't have a camera, so she has to borrow one.

- -

6 He doesn't know the route, so he is confused.

- -

7 They run around the classroom, so I can't focus on my studies.

- -

8 You are busy, so you can't spend time with your family.

- -

Tips for Writing

If절을 문장의 앞에 쓸
때는 뒤에 쉼표(,)를
써서 주절과 구분해
준다.

B 보기에서 알맞은 표현을 찾아 우리말에 맞게 영어로 쓰시오.

1 다시 태어날 수 있다면 나는 의사가 될 텐데.
　　_____

2 졸리지 않다면 나는 그 영화를 볼 수 있을 텐데.
　　_____

3 그 가수가 콘서트를 한다면 나는 티켓을 살 텐데.
　　_____

4 Lisa가 우리 집 근처에 산다면 우리는 매일 만날 텐데.
　　_____

5 비가 오지 않으면 우리는 정원에서 저녁을 먹을 수 있을 텐데.
　　_____

6 Brandon이 그녀의 전화번호를 안다면 그녀에게 전화할 텐데.
　　_____

rain
be born
live near
know
be sleepy
have a concert

C 그림을 보고 각 보기에서 알맞은 표현을 찾아 주어진 상황을 가정하는 문장을 쓰시오.

make	ride on	change into	see

a bird	an igloo	polar bears	a magic broom

0
Imagine that you want to be a TV star.
If I were a TV star, I would receive a lot of presents.
If I were a TV star, I would appear on television.

1
Imagine that you want to be a wizard.
1) _____
2) _____

2
Imagine that you want to explore the North Pole.
1) _____
2) _____

UNIT 2 주요 가정법

Wendy is a good girl. I wish Wendy would live with me in Neverland.
But Tinker Bell talks as if she were a bad girl.

1 〈I wish+가정법 과거〉는 '~(이)라면 좋을 텐데'의 의미로 현재 이루기 힘든 소망을 나타낼 때 쓴다.
I wish I were smart enough to get a perfect score.

2 〈as if+가정법 과거〉는 '마치 ~인 것처럼'의 의미로 현재 사실과 반대되는 내용을 가정할 때 쓴다.
He talks **as if** he **knew** me very well.

A 문장을 다음과 같이 완성하시오.

0 I am sorry I can't afford to buy a new watch.

I wish I could afford to buy a new watch.

0 He acts as if it were his last opportunity.

In fact, it is not his last opportunity.

1 I am sorry Sam doesn't listen to others' opinions.

....

2 I am sorry I am not good at singing.

....

3 I am sorry I don't have a sister to play with.

....

4 I am sorry I can't remember his name.

....

5 He acts ....

In fact, he isn't the president of the club.

6 They speak ....

In fact, they don't know the suspect.

7 She behaves ....

In fact, she can't solve the problem.

8 Angela talks ....

In fact, she isn't my teacher.

94

B 보기에서 알맞은 표현을 찾아 우리말에 맞게 영어로 쓰시오.

1 네가 프랑스어를 할 수 있다면 좋을 텐데.

2 내가 내 남동생보다 키다 크다면 좋을 텐데.

3 나의 아버지가 게임 회사에서 일하면 좋을 텐데.

4 Ellie는 마치 그녀가 일이 많은 것처럼 행동한다.

5 내가 나의 할머니 댁에 방문할 수 있다면 좋을 텐데.

6 그는 마치 내가 그를 시샘하는 것처럼 말한다.

7 Mrs. Brown은 마치 내가 그녀의 딸인 것처럼 나를 대한다.

> have
> speak
> be jealous of
> be tall
> work for
> visit
> treat

C 친구와 문자 메시지를 주고받고 있다. 괄호 안의 표현을 활용하여 문자 메시지를 쓰시오.

0

How about going to see a baseball game?

I can't. I wish I could go to see a baseball game with you.

Why can't you?

My mother is making me clean the bathroom today. She acts as if it were easy. (be easy)

1

How about swimming in the pool?

I can't. 1) _____

Why can't you?

My father asked me to shop for groceries. 2) _____ (have no time)

2

How about reading books in the library?

I can't. 1) _____

Why can't you?

I have to take care of my sister. 2) _____ (be a baby)

WRAP UP

A   다음은 학교의 체육 수업 모습이다. 보기에서 알맞은 표현을 찾아 그림 속 인물들에 대한 문장을 쓰시오.

fly in the sky	be a student	be a model	jump rope

0   Victoria acts as if she had a headache.

1   Mrs. Smith makes noise ....

2   Brian feels ....

3   Jack behaves ....

4   Emma walks ....

B   각 보기에서 알맞은 표현을 찾아 소망을 나타내는 문장을 쓰시오.

buy	save	learn	do

how to dance	money	more clothes	some volunteer work

0   I am always busy. I wish I could have some time to relax.

1   I am short of money.

2   I am not good at dancing.

3   I want to help the poor.

4   I don't have enough clothes to wear.

96

C 다음 우리말에 맞게 영어로 쓰시오.

1

내가 새 신발을 산다면 빨리 달릴 수 있을 텐데.

2

내가 부산에 산다면 매일 바다에서 수영할 텐데.

3

내가 세계 일주를 할 수 있다면 좋을 텐데. (travel around the world)

4

오늘이 일요일이라면 나는 학교에 가지 않을 텐데.

5

Gina는 그녀가 마치 부자인 것처럼 돈을 쓴다.

6

내게 잘생긴 남자 친구가 있다면 좋을 텐데.

D 다음 우리말에 맞게 영어로 쓰시오.

1

I have an older sister. We get along well, but sometimes I can't understand her. She often comes home late. 1) 그녀가 집에 일찍 온다면 나의 부모님이 그녀를 걱정하지 않을 텐데. And she always breaks her promises. 2) 그녀가 약속을 지키면 좋을 텐데.

1) _____ (worry about)

2) _____ (keep)

2

Dear Minhye,

How's life in Sydney? 1) 내가 시드니에 간다면 우리는 함께 오페라 하우스에 갈 수 있을 텐데. Our class misses you very much. 2) 내가 너와 함께 학교에 다닐 수 있다면 좋을 텐데.
Take Care.

Minjun

1) _____

2) _____

E 다음은 인터넷 상담 사이트에 게시된 글이다. 괄호 안의 표현을 활용하여 고민을 상담하는 글을 쓰시오.

0

Anna: I want to dance well like my friend.
She dances as if she were a professional dancer.

Grace: If I were you, I would attend a dance class.

1

Eric: I can't sleep because of my brother.
1) He keeps singing _____. (a rock singer)

Grace: 2) _____ (use earplugs)

2

Alicia: I can't concentrate on my studies.
1) I keep checking my phone _____. (a text message)

Grace: 2) _____ (turn off, for a while)

F 보기에서 알맞은 표현을 찾아 과거로 여행할 수 있다면 하고 싶은 일에 대해 쓰시오.

- Where to go: the Jurassic age, the Joseon Dynasty
- What to do: see real dinosaurs, meet King Sejong

0 If I could travel to the past, I would go to ancient Greece.

I wish I could watch the first Olympic Games.

1 1) _____

2) _____

2 1) _____

2) _____

LESSON 12
분사

run away	follow	lie	knee
newspaper	fold	come up to	propose
doorbell	fix	return	accept
set the table	beside	magazine	amazing
favorite	pocket	blow out	spin
finish	go out	see off	ankle
swing	hang	red pepper paste	attempt
look around	cross	bowl	glide
jump with joy	beat	a spoonful of	gracefully
carry	display	frown	moment

UNIT 1 분사구문의 기본 형태와 의미

Thinking of her mother, Wendy decided to go back home.

★ 분사구문은 부사절(접속사+주어+동사)을 현재분사(v-ing)로 시작하는
부사구로 나타낸 것으로 문장을 간결하고 생동감 있게 표현하고자 할 때
쓴다.

Walking to school, I met my teacher.
Listening to music, Mike cleaned his desk.
Closing the door, Amy started to cry.

Note
1 분사구문은 시간,
  부대상황(동시동작, 연속동작)
  이외에도 이유, 조건, 양보 등의
  의미를 나타낸다.
2 분사구문 만드는 방법
  1) 접속사를 없앤다.
  2) 부사절의 주어를 뺀다.
  3) 부사절의 동사를 v-ing로
     바꾼다.

A 밑줄 친 부분을 분사구문으로 바꿔서 문장을 다시 쓰시오.

1 <u>When she saw me</u>, she ran away.

2 <u>While he was walking to school</u>, Robert was talking with his friend.

3 <u>As she took a walk</u>, Anne talked on the phone.

4 <u>As she ate breakfast</u>, Christine read the newspaper.

5 <u>If you visit their website</u>, you can find more information.

6 <u>While she was cooking dinner</u>, Ashley heard the doorbell ring.

7 <u>As he was setting the table</u>, he sang his favorite song.

8 <u>While I was staying at my uncle's house</u>, I finished the book.

9 <u>If you join the book club</u>, you must read a lot of books.

B 각 보기에서 알맞은 표현을 찾아 우리말에 맞게 영어로 쓰시오.

turn	
hear	
listen to	
turn on	
feel tired	
swing one's arms	
open	

1 팔을 흔들면서, Lily는 그 무대 위에서 춤을 췄다.

----

2 왼쪽으로 돌면, 너는 그 꽃집을 볼 것이다.

----

3 피곤함을 느껴서, 나는 일찍 잠자리에 들었다.

----

check	
go to bed	
see	
study	
look around	
jump with joy	
dance	

4 문을 열면서, Lauren은 교실을 둘러보았다.

----

5 그 소식을 들었을 때, John은 기뻐서 날뛰었다.

----

6 라디오를 들으면서, 나는 수학 공부를 했다.

----

7 내 휴대 전화를 켜고, 나는 문자 메시지들을 확인했다.

C 그림을 보고 괄호 안의 표현을 활용하여 그림 속 인물들의 행동을 나타내는 문장을 쓰시오.

0 (watch, clean, sing)

Watching TV, Mr. Scott is cleaning the floor.

Cleaning the floor, Mr. Scott is singing.

1  (carry, talk, run to school)

1) ---

2) ---

2  (wait for, listen to, eat)

1) ---

2) ---

UNIT 2 with + (대)명사 + 분사

I left Wendy with tears falling from my eyes.

★ 〈with+(대)명사+분사〉는 '~을 …한 채로'의 의미로 (대)명사의 동작이나 상태를 설명한다. (대)명사와 분사의 관계가 능동이면 현재분사를, 수동이면 과거분사를 쓴다.

Anna cried **with her lower lip shaking**.
The actor entered the airport **with his fans following him**.
My mother scolded me **with her arms folded**.
James listened to music **with his eyes closed**.

> **Note**
> 〈with+(대)명사+형용사/부사/전치사구〉로도 '~을 …한 채로'의 의미를 나타낼 수 있다.
> The manager spoke **with his mouth full**.
> I fell asleep **with the TV on**.
> **With so many children in the park**, it was noisy.

A 문장을 다음과 같이 고쳐 쓰시오.

0 As he ate lunch, his eyes were fixed on the table.

    He ate lunch with his eyes fixed on the table.

1 The bird flew away. Its leg was broken.

2 Morgan ate a hamburger while her baby was sleeping beside her.

3 Paul left home. The windows were open.

4 As Alex talked to his teacher, his hands were in his pockets.

5 As night was coming on, it became dark.

6 Seven dogs were born. Their eyes were closed.

7 The snow was falling hard. Ted didn't go out.

8 The monkey was hanging on the tree. Its legs were swinging.

B 각 보기에서 알맞은 표현을 찾아 우리말에 맞게 영어로 쓰시오.

1 John은 머리카락을 자른 채로 학교에 왔다.

_____

2 입을 다문 채로 쿠키를 먹어라.

_____

3 Daniel은 다리를 꼰 채로 잠이 들었다.

_____

4 Julia는 그녀의 개가 그녀를 뒤따르는 채로 뛰고 있었다.

_____

5 Emily는 심장이 빠르게 뛰는 채로 David를 기다렸다.

_____

6 Bill은 오른쪽 팔이 부러진 채로 집에 왔다.

_____

7 그 책은 몇몇 페이지가 사라진 채로 진열되었다.

_____

eat
run
display
wait for
come to
fall asleep
come home

one's hair cut
miss
close
break
cross
follow
beat fast

C 그림을 보고 괄호 안의 표현을 활용하여 동물들의 행동을 나타내는 문장을 쓰시오.

0 The monkey is sitting with its arms folded. _____ (sit, arms)

1 The bear _____ . (lie, legs)

2 The giraffe _____ . (eat leaves, eyes)

3 The crocodile _____ . (swim, mouth)

WRAP UP

A 그림을 보고 보기에서 알맞은 표현을 찾아, 아들의 행동과 이에 대한 엄마의 당부를 나타내는 문장을 쓰시오.

eat lunch	the computer on	one's shoes on
one's mouth full	wear one's shoes	

1

Using the computer, he falls asleep.

1) "Don't sleep with _____."

2

1) _____, he speaks to his mother.

2) _____

3

1) _____, he walks around the house.

2) _____

B 그림을 보고 보기에서 알맞은 표현을 찾아 Susie와 고양이의 행동을 묘사하는 문장을 쓰시오.

0 **1** **2** **3**

cry	return home	find	carry
come up to	walk down the street		

0 Putting on her coat, Susie went out.

1 _____

2 _____

3 _____

C 다음 우리말에 맞게 영어로 쓰시오.

1

길을 따라 걷다가, 나는 나의 영어 선생님을 만났다. (along the street)

2

Taylor는 어젯밤에 TV를 켜 놓은 채로 잠들었다.

3

의자에 앉아서, 그녀는 패션 잡지를 읽었다.

4

그녀는 눈을 감은 채로 그 촛불들을 불어서 껐다. (blow out)

5

나의 집을 지나가면서, Pamela는 내 이름을 불렀다. (pass by)

6

Ben은 다리를 꼰 채 소파에 앉아 있었다.

7

피곤함을 느껴서, Sam은 그의 남동생을 배웅하러 공항에 가지 않았다. (see one's brother off)

D 다음 우리말에 맞게 영어로 쓰시오.

1

Mike was hungry. So he decided to make *bibimbap*. He put rice, vegetables and red pepper paste in a bowl. 1) 노래를 부르면서, 그는 그것들을 함께 섞었다. Then, it was time to eat. 2) 비빔밥을 한 숟가락 먹으면서, 그는 얼굴을 찡그렸다. It was too spicy!

1) _____ (mix)

2) _____ (a spoonful of, frown)

2

Today, I saw something interesting at the park. A man and a woman were sitting on a bench. Suddenly, the man got down on one knee. 1) 그녀에게 반지를 주며, 그는 그녀에게 프러포즈를 했다. 2) 눈에 눈물을 머금은 채, 그녀는 그 반지를 받았다.

1) _____

2) _____ (accept)

E 그림을 보고 주어진 표현을 활용하여 피겨 스케이팅 경기 관람 후기를 쓰시오.

1

- do an amazing spin

2

- fall down

3

- stand up and glide gracefully

a smile on one's face   attempt a triple jump
hold one ankle above one's head

> *September 9th*
>
> **I went to the ice rink to see the figure skating championships. My favorite skater Ella took 2nd place.**
>
> **1 She** _____ .
>
> **2 But** _____ .
>
> **3 Soon** _____ .
>
> **It was a touching moment.**

F 주어진 표현을 활용하여 그림 1, 2가 나타내는 상황을 묘사하고, 그에 알맞은 그림 3의 내용을 추론하여 쓰시오.

1

- take one's bag
- run away

2

- run after
- catch him

3

- get one's bag back
- thank the man

1 _____, a thief ran away.

2 _____

3 _____

106

SECTION 3
PATTERNS FOR WRITING

Useful Patterns for Writing 1

★ 주어+means ~: ~는 …을 의미한다
His family means everything to him.

★ Please let me ~: 제가 ~하게 해 주세요
Please let me buy you dinner this time.

1 친구가 된다는 것은 서로를 믿는다는 것을 의미한다. (*trust: 믿다)

2 제가 당신과 함께 가도록 해 주세요.

3 많은 문화에서 깨진 거울은 불운을 의미한다.

4 제가 당신의 휴대 전화를 사용하도록 해 주세요.

5 어른이 된다는 것은 너의 행동들에 책임을 지는 것을 의미한다. (*responsibility: 책임)

6 당신의 이메일 주소를 제게 알려 주세요.

7 성공이 돈을 많이 버는 것을 의미하지는 않는다.

8 제 상황을 설명하게 해 주세요.

9 빨간색은 중국인에게 부와 행운을 의미한다. (*fortune: 부(富))

10 당신의 최종 결정을 제게 알려 주세요. (*final: 최종의)

Useful Patterns *for Writing* 2

★ refer to ~: ~을 나타내다
The star **refers to** terms for an advanced learner.

★ I am (quite[fairly, absolutely]) sure[certain] ~: 저는 ~을 (꽤[상당히, 전적으로]) 확신합니다
I am quite sure that you'll pass the driving test.

---

1   이 문장에서, '그것'은 지구 온난화를 나타낸다. (*global warming: 지구 온난화)

----

2   나는 우리 팀이 이 경기에서 이길 것이라고 확신한다.

----

3   이 수치들은 각 학교의 학생 수를 나타낸다. (*figure: 수치)

----

4   나는 그가 곧 사과할 것이라고 꽤 확신한다.

----

5   '채식주의자'라는 단어는 고기를 먹지 않는 사람을 나타낸다. (*vegetarian: 채식주의자)

----

6   나는 이 에세이를 오늘 끝낼 수 있을지 확신하지 못한다.

----

7   밑줄 친 문장은 무엇을 나타내니?

----

8   나는 그녀가 곧 돌아올 것이라고 전적으로 확신한다.

----

9   '생물학'이라는 용어는 살아 있는 것들에 대한 학문을 나타낸다. (*biology: 생물학)

----

10 나는 그가 시험공부를 했는지 그다지 확신하지 못한다.

Useful Patterns for Writing 3

★ In my opinion, ~: 내 생각에는 ~
In my opinion, he is a successful businessman.

★ 주어+(can) be defined as ~: ~는 …로 정의된다(정의될 수 있다)
Success **can be defined as** achieving a goal.

1 내 생각에는 그가 그의 시간을 낭비하고 있다.

2 언어는 의사소통의 체계로 정의될 수 있다. (*system: 체계)

3 내 생각에는 네게 그 실패에 대한 책임이 있다. (*responsible for: ~에 책임이 있는)

4 가족은 서로 친척 관계인 한 무리의 사람들로 정의된다. (*related to: ~와 친척 관계인)

5 내 생각에는 그가 심각한 실수를 했다.

6 취미는 사람들이 즐거움을 위해 정기적으로 하는 활동으로 정의된다.

7 내 생각에는 그녀에 대한 그 소문들은 사실이 아니다.

8 녹색 일자리는 환경을 보호하는 일자리로 정의될 수 있다. (*a green job: 녹색 일자리)

9 내 생각에는 컴퓨터가 우리의 삶을 더 복잡하게 만든다.

10 다른 사람의 신분증을 사용하는 것은 절도로 정의될 수 있다. (*ID: 신분증, theft: 절도)

Useful Patterns for Writing 4

★ I wonder if I could ~: 내가 ~해도 되는지 궁금하다
I wonder if I could talk to you for a few minutes.

★ It seems to me ~: 내가 보기에 ~인 것 같다
It seems to me that he is a liar.

1 내가 네 컴퓨터를 써도 되는지 궁금하다.

2 내가 보기에 아무도 저 오래된 집에 살지 않는 것 같다.

3 네가 내게 수학을 가르쳐 줄 수 있는지 궁금하다.

4 내가 보기에 너는 나를 더 이상 믿지 않는 것 같다.

5 내가 이 의자를 옮기는 걸 네가 도와줄 수 있는지 궁금하다.

6 내가 보기에 그 도둑은 남자가 아니었던 것 같다.

7 내가 너에게 질문 몇 가지를 해도 되는지 궁금하다.

8 내가 보기에 그는 좋은 야구 선수인 것 같다.

9 지금 네가 나를 집에 데려다 줄 수 있는지 궁금하다

10 내가 보기에 그 대통령은 아주 인기가 많은 것 같다. (*president: 대통령)

Useful Patterns for Writing 5

★ I appreciate ~: 나는 ~에 감사한다
  I appreciate all your help last weekend.

★ I apologize for ~: 나는 ~에 대해 사과한다
  I apologize for what I did yesterday.

1 저는 제 질문에 대한 당신의 친절한 답변에 정말 감사드립니다.

2 저는 이로 인해 일어날지 모를 불편에 대해 사과드립니다. (*inconvenience: 불편)

3 우리는 우리 동아리에 대한 여러분의 관심에 감사드립니다.

4 저는 오늘 아침 당신에게 말했던 것에 대해 사과드립니다.

5 저는 이 문제에 대한 당신의 이해에 감사드립니다. (*matter: 문제)

6 저희는 그 버스의 늦은 도착에 대해 사과드립니다. (*arrival: 도착)

7 저희는 당신의 시간과 노력에 감사드립니다.

8 저는 당신의 편지에 답하는 것이 지연된 점에 대해 사과드립니다. (*delay: 지연)

9 저는 당신이 이 웹 사이트를 만드는 일에 도움 주신 것에 감사드립니다.

10 저는 당신을 밖에서 기다리게 한 것에 대해 사과드립니다.

Useful Patterns for Writing 6

★ spend money[time] v-ing: ~하는 데 돈[시간]을 쓰다
They spend a lot of money eating out on weekends.

★ waste money[time] v-ing: ~하는 데 돈[시간]을 낭비하다
She is wasting a lot of time chatting online.

1 나는 인터넷을 검색하는 데 시간을 보내는 걸 좋아한다.

2 너는 입을 옷을 고르는 데 네 시간을 낭비하고 있다.

3 그는 그의 집을 개조하는 데 그의 돈 대부분을 썼다. (*remodel: 개조하다)

4 그는 Jim과 어울리는 데 많은 시간을 낭비했다. (*hang around with: ~와 어울리다)

5 나는 요즘 운동하는 데 내 시간의 대부분을 보낸다.

6 나는 지루한 영화를 보는 데 돈을 낭비했다.

7 그들은 그 제품을 광고하는 데 더 많은 돈을 쓰길 원한다. (*advertise: 광고하다)

8 우리는 어제 택시를 기다리는 데 시간을 낭비했다.

9 그녀는 꽃을 돌보는 데 그녀의 여가를 보낸다. (*spare time: 여가)

10 나는 사용하지도 않을 펜을 사는 데 돈을 낭비하고 싶지 않다.

Useful Patterns for Writing 7

★ would rather A than B: B하느니 차라리 A하겠다
   I **would rather go out with her than stay home**.

★ cannot help v-ing: ~하지 않을 수 없다, ~할 수밖에 없다
   I **could not help laughing** at his funny jokes.

1 나는 붐비는 버스를 타느니 차라리 택시를 타겠다. (*crowded: 붐비는)

2 나는 그의 결정에 동의하지 않을 수 없었다. (*agree with: ~에 동의하다)

3 나는 네 도움을 요청하느니 차라리 그것을 혼자 하겠다.

4 나는 그녀에 대한 내 진짜 감정을 숨길 수밖에 없다.

5 나는 지루한 책을 읽느니 차라리 잠을 자겠다.

6 우리는 우리의 실수를 인정할 수밖에 없었다. (*admit: 인정하다)

7 나는 춤을 추느니 차라리 노래를 한 곡 부르겠다.

8 나는 초콜릿을 보면 그것을 먹지 않을 수 없다.

9 나는 저 낡은 재킷을 입느니 차라리 추운 게 낫다.

10 나는 영화에 대한 그의 열정을 존경하지 않을 수 없었다. (*passion for: ~에 대한 열정)

Useful Patterns *for Writing* 8

★ I know how to-v: 나는 ~하는 방법을 안다
She **knew how to fix** the broken bike.

★ be anxious to-v: ~을 간절히 바라다
Everyone **was anxious to know** the winner of the game.

---

1   그들은 그 환경 문제를 해결하는 방법을 안다. (*environmental: 환경의)

2   그는 조용한 장소에서 살기를 간절히 바란다.

3   나는 건강한 방식으로 살을 빼는 방법을 안다.

4   그녀는 자신의 방을 가지길 간절히 바란다.

5   그는 좋은 첫인상을 주는 방법을 안다. (*first impression: 첫인상)

6   나는 나의 가족과 함께 세계 일주를 하길 간절히 바란다.

7   그녀는 그녀의 부모님을 행복하게 만드는 방법을 안다.

8   우리는 누가 우릴 가르칠지 알기를 간절히 바란다.

9   나는 이 게임을 하는 방법을 모른다.

10 그들은 공항에 제시간에 도착하기를 간절히 바란다.

Useful Patterns for Writing 9

★ as+원급+as ~ that has ever v-ed: 지금까지 ~에 못지않게 …한
He is **as fast as** any runner **that has ever run**.

★ no longer / not ~ any longer: 더 이상 ~않다
It is **no longer** possible to change your reservation.
It is **not** possible to change your reservation **any longer**.

1 그는 지금까지 경기했던 어느 운동선수에 못지않게 힘이 세다.

2 나는 더 이상 그의 무례한 행동을 참을 수 없다. (*stand: 참다)

3 그녀는 지금까지 살았던 어느 예술가에 못지않게 훌륭하다.

4 사람들은 더 이상 공공장소에서 담배 피우는 것이 허락되지 않는다.

5 그녀는 지금까지 살았던 어느 정치인에 못지않게 정직하다. (*politician: 정치인)

6 그 회사는 스포츠카를 더 이상 생산하길 원하지 않는다.

7 그는 지금까지 경기했던 어느 테니스 선수에 못지않게 재능이 있다.

8 그는 더 이상 그의 형과 싸우고 싶어 하지 않는다.

9 그 노래는 지금까지 불려졌던 어느 노래에 못지않게 훌륭하다.

10 그녀는 더 이상 다른 사람들의 의견을 신경 쓰지 않는다.

Useful Patterns *for Writing 10*

★ the+최상급+주어+have ever v-ed: ~가 지금까지 ~한 중에 가장 …한
This is the most beautiful island I have ever seen.

★ have a hard time v-ing: ~하는 데 힘든 시간을 보내다, ~하는 데 애를 먹다
She had a hard time sleeping at night.

1 그는 내가 지금까지 만나 본 중에 가장 성공한 사람이다.

2 우리는 점심으로 무엇을 먹을지 결정하는 데 애를 먹었다.

3 이 판타지 소설은 내가 지금까지 읽어 본 중에 가장 지루한 책이다.

4 그는 어제 그 제과점을 찾는 데 애를 먹었다.

5 이것은 내가 지금까지 맛본 중에 가장 맛있는 볶음밥이다. (*fried rice: 볶음밥)

6 나는 그 강의를 이해하는 데 힘든 시간을 보내고 있다. (*lecture: 강의)

7 이 뮤지컬은 내가 지금까지 본 것 중 가장 훌륭한 공연이다. (*performance: 공연)

8 그녀는 그녀의 블로그를 만드는 데 애를 먹고 있다. (*set up: 만들다)

9 이 여행은 지금까지 우리가 했던 경험 중 가장 값진 경험이 될 것이다. (*valuable: 값진)

10 그들은 택시를 잡는 데 애를 먹었다.

Useful Patterns for Writing 11

★ If I were you, I would ~: 내가 너라면, ~할 텐데
  If I were you, **I would** not accept his invitation.

★ If it were not for ~: ~이 없다면
  If it were not for water, we could not live.

1 내가 너라면, 일찍 잠자리에 들 텐데.

2 시험이 없다면, 나는 스트레스를 받지 않을 텐데. (*feel stressed: 스트레스를 받다)

3 내가 너라면, 결코 희망을 포기하지 않을 텐데.

4 인터넷이 없다면, 우리의 생활이 매우 다를 텐데.

5 내가 너라면, 밤에 더 천천히 운전할 텐데.

6 비가 오지 않는다면, 우리는 우리의 여행을 즐길 수 있을 텐데.

7 내가 너라면, 그런 비싼 호텔에 머물지 않을 텐데.

8 오븐이 없다면, 나는 빵을 굽지 못할 텐데.

9 내가 너라면, 나의 선생님과 상의할 텐데. (*consult with: ~와 상의하다)

10 내 친구들이 없다면, 나는 때때로 외로울 텐데.

Useful Patterns *for Writing* 12

★ I told him not to-v ~: 나는 그에게 ~하지 말라고 말했다
  I **told him not to turn on** the air conditioner.

★ It is probable[likely, possible] that[to] ~: ~할 것 같다[~할 가능성이 있다]
  It is probable that he will cancel his trip.

1 나는 그녀에게 그녀의 시험 점수에 대해 걱정하지 말라고 말했다.

2 더 많은 관광객들이 내년에 그 나라를 방문할 것 같다.

3 그는 내게 그의 집에 내 애완동물을 데리고 오지 말라고 말했다.

4 이 궂은 날씨에 그 산에 올라가는 것은 가능하지 않다.

5 나는 그녀에게 Jake를 크리스마스 파티에 초대하지 말라고 말했다.

6 그녀가 플루트 대회에서 우승할 것 같다. (*competition: 대회)

7 그녀는 우리에게 그 중요한 서류를 만지지 말라고 말했다. (*document: 서류)

8 지금 너의 결정을 바꾸는 것은 가능하다.

9 나는 그녀에게 그 실수에 대해 내게 사과하지 말라고 말했다.

10 그들이 곧 그 실험 결과를 발표할 것 같다. (*announce: 발표하다)

WORD LIST

LESSON 1

brush one's teeth 이를 닦다
comfortable 편안한
borrow 빌리다
be satisfied with ~에 만족하다
score 점수

—

announcer 아나운서, 방송 진행자
lend 빌려 주다
author 작가, 저자
anger 화, 분노
invitation 초대(장)

—

behavior 행동
impolite 무례한
refreshed (기분이) 상쾌한
embarrassed 당황스러운, 난처한
furniture 가구

—

excited 신이 난
perm 파마하다
repair 고치다, 수리하다
fire 발사하다
steal 훔치다

—

sweep 쓸다
floor 바닥
shake 흔들리다, 흔들다
badly 심하게, 몹시
fall down 넘어지다

—

stressed 스트레스를 받는
point at ~을 가리키다
costume 의상
director 감독, 책임자
announce 발표하다, 알리다

—

whisper 속삭이다
take a walk 산책하다
information 정보
witness 목격자
statement 진술

—

pass by (옆을) 지나가다
trip 여행
water sports 수상 스포츠
vacation 방학, 휴가
volunteer 자원봉사의

LESSON 2

wake up 깨우다
practice 연습하다
have a cold 감기에 걸리다
remind 상기시키다
already 이미, 벌써

—

full 배부른, 가득한
take a shower 샤워하다
ring (전화가) 울리다
trust 믿다, 신뢰하다
lift 들어 올리다

—

boring 지루한
fall asleep 잠들다
catch up with ~을 따라잡다
festival 축제
rice 쌀, 밥

—

stew 스튜
contact 연락하다
mentor 멘토, 충실한 조언자
refund 환불(금)
necklace 목걸이

—

earring 귀걸이
cheerful 쾌활한, 신이 나는
take part in ~에 참가하다
palm 손바닥
display 전시

—

turn off ~을 끄다
flash 플래시
take a picture 사진을 찍다
treat 다루다, 취급하다
with care 조심하여

—

stretch 뻗다, 스트레칭 하다
go camping 캠핑 가다
toothache 치통
terrible 형편없는, 끔찍한
burn 데다, 불에 타다

—

tongue 혀
hole 구멍
go on a picnic 소풍 가다
broken 고장 난
sneakers 운동화

LESSON 3

clothing 옷, 의복
manner 태도, 예의
novel 소설
useful 유용한
stripe 줄무늬

exchange 교환하다
look for ~을 찾다
cartoon 만화
smelly 냄새나는
loudly 큰 소리로

recommend 추천하다
language 언어
be familiar with ~에 익숙하다
introduce 소개하다
respect 존경하다

correct 맞는, 옳은
fancy 고급의, 근사한
for the first time 처음으로
laugh at ~을 비웃다
be born 태어나다

reserve 예약하다
childhood 어린 시절
solve 풀다, 해결하다
explain 설명하다
attend 참석하다

disagree 동의하지 않다
opinion 의견
peel 껍질을 벗기다
hold (파티 등을) 열다, 개최하다
park 주차하다

disappointed 실망한
price tag 가격표
be tired of ~에 싫증이 나다
a variety of 다양한 ~
offer 제공하다

discounted 할인된
outlet 할인점, 아울렛
provide 제공하다
unlimited 무제한의
gallery 미술관, 화랑

LESSON 4

enough 충분한
matter 중요하다
wonder 궁금하다
earth 지구
certain 확실한, 틀림없는

tell a lie 거짓말하다
married 결혼을 한
important 중요한
strange 이상한
hurt 다치게 하다, 아프다

empty 비어 있는, 빈
interview 인터뷰를 하다
wait in line 줄을 서서 기다리다
pour 붓다, 따르다
display 진열하다

rumor 소문
turn out 드러나다, 밝혀지다
false 틀린, 사실이 아닌
surround 둘러싸다
receive 받다

place 놓다, 설치하다
ashamed 부끄러운
lose (시합 등에서) 지다
liar 거짓말쟁이
contest 대회, 시합

twist (발목·손목 등을) 삐다
ankle 발목
participate in ~에 참가하다
decorate 장식하다
work of art 예술품

museum 박물관, 미술관
camel 낙타
desert 사막
fashionable 유행하는, 유행을 따른
confident 자신감 있는

impression 인상
play a role 역할을 하다
gain 얻다
popularity 인기
appearance (겉)모습, 외모

LESSON 5

driver's license 운전 면허증
remember 기억하다
on time 시간에 맞게, 정시에
drugstore 약국
nearby 가까운 곳에

—

be interested in ~에 관심이 있다
eat out 외식하다
wallet 지갑
free 무료의
broadcasting 방송(업)

—

interviewer 면접관
apply 지원하다
skill 기량, 기술
grocery store 식료품점
stay 머무르다

—

attach 붙이다
hold (회의·시합 등을) 열다
on foot 걸어서
performance 공연
sculpture 조각품

—

tour 관광
souvenir 기념품
leave for ~로 떠나다
cavity 충치
prevent 막다, 예방하다

—

eyesight 시력
maintain 유지하다, 지키다
get over 극복하다
nail 못
hammer 망치

—

gather 모이다
forget 잊다
somewhere 어딘가에(서)
after a while 잠시 후
refund 환불(금)

—

deliver 배달하다
auditorium 강당
take part in ~에 참여하다
cafeteria 식당, 카페테리아
main entrance 정문, 중앙 출입구

LESSON 6

east 동쪽
usually 보통, 대개
recommend 추천하다
freeze 얼다
degree (온도 단위인) 도

—

boil 끓다
practice 연습하다
through ~을 통해
telescope 망원경
attend 참석하다, 다니다

—

second 두 번째의
medicine 약
author 작가, 저자
award 상
put on ~을 입다, 신다

—

wash the dishes 설거지하다
review 복습하다
delicious 맛있는
vet 수의사
treat 치료하다

—

barber 이발사
parrot 앵무새
do yoga 요가를 하다
relieve 완화시키다
far away 멀리 떨어져

—

experiment 실험
dangerous 위험한
make a mistake 실수하다
work 작동되다
break 고장 나다

—

detergent 세제
protect 보호하다
environment 환경
charge 충전하다
take a rest 휴식을 취하다

—

volunteer 자원봉사로 하다
trick 속임수, 마술
local 지역의
foreigner 외국인
comfortable 편안한

LESSON 7

pay attention to ~에 집중하다
keep a diary 일기를 쓰다
suit 정장
bake (음식을) 굽다
truth 사실, 진실

fever 열
medicine 약
get lost 길을 잃다
downtown 시내에, 번화가에
fail an exam 시험에 떨어지다

write down 적어 두다
apologize 사과하다
accident 사고
appointment 약속
expect 기대하다

annoyed 짜증이 난
bored 지루해 하는
get along with ~와 잘 지내다
efficiently 효율적으로
spill 쏟다, 엎지르다

skip 거르다, 빼먹다
mud 진흙
discuss 토론하다
various 다양한
accept 받아들이다

proposal 제안
have a sore throat 목감기에 걸리다
advertisement 광고
sew 바느질하다
thread 실

jewelry 보석류
robbery 강도 (사건)
theft 절도
track (자동차 바퀴) 자국
escape 달아나다, 탈출하다

wig 가발
bald 대머리의, 머리가 벗겨진
pursue 추적하다, 뒤쫓다
suspect 용의자
earthquake 지진

LESSON 8

vegetable 채소
rocking chair 흔들의자
next 그 다음에
update 갱신하다, 업데이트하다
decide 결정하다

invite 초대하다
take care of ~을 돌보다
machine 기계
vote 투표하다
take a trip 여행하다

holiday 휴가
save 절약하다, 아끼다
energy 에너지
for a long time 오랫동안
understand 이해하다

attractive 매력적인
blind 눈이 먼, 맹인인
lucky 운이 좋은
zookeeper 동물원 사육사
play 연극

amazed 놀란
match 경기, 시합
express 나타내다, 표현하다
feeling 느낌, 기분
upset 속상한, 언짢은

racehorse 경주마
audience 청중, 관중
direction 방향
friendship 우정
stand up 일어나다

lose weight 살이 빠지다, 살을 빼다
relieve 완화시키다
farewell party 송별회
bring 가져오다
friendly 친절한, 다정한

responsible 책임감 있는
costly 많은 비용이 드는
regularly 규칙적으로
feed 밥을 먹이다, 먹이를 주다
smelly 냄새나는

LESSON 9

previous 이전의
laptop 휴대용 컴퓨터, 노트북
climb 오르다
strict 엄격한
complicated 복잡한

worry 걱정하다
grade 성적, 점수
attention 보살핌, 관심
throw 던지다
far 멀리

novel 소설
dish 요리
storm 폭풍
scene 장면
voice 목소리

stylish 세련된, 멋진
weight 무게, 체중
thickness 두께
storage 저장
capacity 용량

athlete 운동선수
respected 존경받는, 높이 평가되는
generous 관대한
experience 경험
bright 밝은

cheerful 쾌활한
notice ~을 알아차리다
focus on ~에 주의를 집중하다
terrible 끔찍한
downtown 시내에

believe 믿다
recycle 재활용하다
throw away 버리다
trash 쓰레기
intelligent 총명한, 똑똑한

energetic 활동적인
activity 활동
useful 유용한, 도움이 되는
discussion 논의
creative 창의적인

LESSON 10

own 자신의
so far 지금까지
yet 아직
during ~ 동안
transfer 옮기다, 전학 가다

price 값, 가격
avoid ~을 하지 않으려 하다, ~을 피하다
waste 낭비하다
electricity 전기, 전력
turn off (전기 등을) 끄다

underwear 속옷
exercise 운동하다
health 건강
the elderly 노인들
station 역, 정거장

wedding 결혼(식)
joke 농담, 우스개
library 도서관
agree with ~에 동의하다
increase 증가하다, 늘다

book 예약하다
opportunity 기회
pose 포즈를 취하다
require 요구하다, 필요로 하다
rotten 썩은

hole 구멍
because of ~ 때문에
lyric (노래의) 가사
experiment 실험
firefighter 소방관

take part in ~에 참여하다
talent 재주, 장기
permission 허락, 허가
choose 선택하다, 고르다
carefully 신중히

character 등장인물
touching 감동적인
faith 믿음, 신뢰
peel (과일 등의) 껍질을 벗기다
in detail 자세히

LESSON 11

headache 두통
marathon 마라톤
route 길, 경로
confused 혼란스러워 하는
spend time with ~와 시간을 보내다

sleepy 졸리운
receive 받다
present 선물
appear (TV 등에) 출현하다, 나타나다
wizard 마법사

broom 빗자루
explore 탐험하다
the North Pole 북극
polar bear 북극곰
igloo 이글루

perfect score 만점
afford to ~할 여유가 있다
opportunity 기회
opinion 의견
suspect 용의자

work for ~에서 일하다
be jealous of ~을 질투하다
shop for groceries 장을 보다
take care of ~을 돌보다
jump rope 줄넘기하다

relax 쉬다, 긴장을 풀다
be short of ~이 부족하다
do volunteer work 자원봉사를 하다
break one's promise 약속을 어기다
professional 전문적인

attend (~에) 다니다
earplug 귀마개
concentrate on ~에 집중하다
text message 문자 메시지
for a while 잠시

past 과거
ancient 고대의
age 시대, 시기
dinosaur 공룡
dynasty 왕조

LESSON 12

run away 달아나다
newspaper 신문
doorbell 초인종
set the table 상을 차리다
favorite 매우 좋아하는

finish 끝내다, 마치다
swing 흔들다
look around 둘러보다
jump with joy 기뻐 날뛰다
carry 들고 있다, 나르다

follow 따라가다, 따라오다
fold 접다
fix 고정시키다
beside 옆에
pocket 호주머니

go out 외출하다
hang 매달리다
cross (팔·다리 따위를) 꼬다
beat (심장이) 고동치다
display 진열하다, 전시하다

lie 누워 있다, 눕다
come up to ~에게 다가가다
return 돌아오다
magazine 잡지
blow out (~을) 불어서 끄다

see off ~을 배웅하다
red pepper paste 고추장
bowl 그릇, 사발
a spoonful of ~ 한 숟가락
frown 얼굴을 찡그리다

knee 무릎
propose 청혼하다, 프러포즈하다
accept 받다, 받아들이다
amazing 놀라운
spin 회전

ankle 발목
attempt 시도하다
glide 미끄러지듯 가다
gracefully 우아하게
moment 순간

지은이

NE능률 영어교육연구소

NE능률 영어교육연구소는 혁신적이며 효율적인 영어 교재를 개발하고
영어 학습의 질을 한 단계 높이고자 노력하는 NE능률의 연구조직입니다.

Writing Builder 3

펴 낸 이 주민홍
펴 낸 곳 서울특별시 마포구 월드컵북로 396(상암동) 누리꿈스퀘어 비즈니스타워 10층
(주)NE능률 (우편번호 03925)
펴 낸 날 2013년 1월 10일 초판 제1쇄 발행
2022년 2월 15일 제13쇄
전 화 02 2014 7114
팩 스 02 3142 0356
홈페이지 www.neungyule.com
등록번호 제 1-68호
I S B N 978-89-6694-540-5 53740
정 가 10,000원

NE 능률

고객센터

교재 내용 문의: contact.nebooks.co.kr (별도의 가입 절차 없이 작성 가능)
제품 구매, 교환, 불량, 반품 문의: 02-2014-7114
☎ 전화문의는 본사 업무시간 중에만 가능합니다.

WRITING BUILDER

정답

3

NE 능률

WRITING BUILDER

정답

3

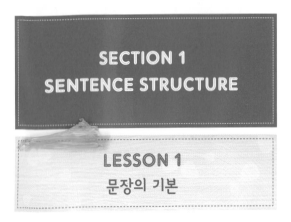

SECTION 1
SENTENCE STRUCTURE

LESSON 1
문장의 기본

UNIT 1
p. 10~11

A

1 The weather is becoming warmer.
2 I bought some bread at the bakery.
3 You should keep your hands clean.
4 Jake showed me his new cell phone.
5 Jessie borrowed a book from the library.
6 Their teacher looks kind and friendly.
7 She was satisfied with her test score.
8 He made his girlfriend a strawberry cake.
9 My parents want me to be an announcer.

B

1 Many people watched the baseball game.
2 Amanda painted the table yellow.
3 She lent me the author's book.
4 His face turned red with anger.
5 I will send Mr. and Mrs. Brown an invitation.
6 Ricky doesn't like his new hairstyle.
7 They think his behavior impolite.

C

1 Yunji[She] couldn't solve the problem and she was embarrassed.
2 Yunji[She] moved some furniture and she was tired.
3 Yunji[She] played a card game (with her friend) and she was excited.

UNIT 2
p. 12~13

A

1 I saw John entering the bank.
2 She had her hair permed at a hair salon.
3 Our teacher made us clean the classroom.
4 She felt everyone looking at her.
5 Julia had her computer repaired yesterday.
6 Some people heard a gun fired across the street.
7 My parents don't let me travel alone.

B

1 Christine had her bag stolen yesterday.

2 His father always makes him sweep the floor.
3 Nobody saw her leaving the room.
4 She heard the music played on the radio.
5 They felt the house shaking badly.
6 I saw my mother cooking bacon.
7 Mr. Jones will let her go to the concert.

C

1 1) A man heard a boy crying.
   2) He let him play with his (soccer) ball.
2 1) A woman smelled some bread burning.
   2) She had a boy open the window.

WRAP UP
p. 14~16

A

1 1) I usually go swimming when I'm stressed.
   2) It makes me feel refreshed.
2 1) I usually read comic books when I'm stressed.
   2) It makes me forget my problems.

B

1 is sweeping the ground
2 are eating ice cream
3 is giving children candy
4 is looking at the theme park map

C

1 Jason became a famous movie director.
2 I lent George 20 dollars[$20] last Wednesday.
3 Her smile always makes me happy.
4 She drinks a cup of coffee every morning.
5 They heard the test score announced.
6 My father had the old car fixed[repaired].
7 I saw Emma whispering to my friend.

D

1 1) I saw Josh taking a walk with his dog yesterday.
   2) But she didn't let me have a dog.
2 1) You can enjoy the beautiful flowers with your family.
   2) You can get more information from our website.

E

1 1) I was cooking in the kitchen.
   2) I felt someone passing by.
2 1) I was watching TV in the living room.
   2) I saw a cat playing with a watch.

F

1 How about learning water sports? It will make your vacation more exciting.
2 How about doing some volunteer work? It will make you a better person.

2

LESSON 2
문장의 확장 I (접속사)

UNIT 1
p. 18~19

A

1 I got up before my mother woke me up.
2 If you want to be a singer, practice hard.
3 When Ben has a cold, he eats chicken soup.
4 They took a taxi because they were very tired.
5 Though it rained hard, the boys played soccer.
6 My father easily forgets things unless I remind him.
7 Maria ate all the potato chips though she was already full.
8 My teacher was angry because I didn't do my homework.

B

1 If it rains tomorrow, we will stay home.
2 Though I have many friends, I am not happy.
3 After he checked his email, he ate breakfast.
4 While we were watching TV, Sam made dinner.

UNIT 2
p. 19~20

A

1 The question was so easy that I could answer it.
2 Mason is such a strong boy that he can lift the desk.
3 The class was so boring that she almost fell asleep.
4 Sophia ran so fast that I could not catch up with her.
5 It was such a great movie that I wanted to see it again.

B

1 Eric is so young that he cannot drive a car.
2 Mrs. Turner is so rich that she can buy anything.

UNIT 3
p. 20~21

A

1 Susie will buy either a jacket or a coat.
2 Neither Bill nor Kate likes action movies.
3 You can contact us by either phone or email.
4 Mr. White is not only my teacher, but also a great mentor. / Mr. White is a great mentor as well as my teacher.
5 Both Jessie and Kevin will come to my birthday party.
6 They gave us not only a full refund but also a free gift. / They gave us a free gift as well as a full refund.

B

1 Jim will eat either pizza or a hamburger.
2 Emma will wear both a necklace and earrings.
3 Brian will study neither math nor history.

WRAP UP
p. 22~24

A

1 It was such a great dessert that I ate it all.
2 It was such a funny game that I couldn't stop laughing.
3 It was such an exciting experience that I told my friend about it.

B

1 1) when you read them
   2) before you enter the library
2 1) when you are in the water
   2) before you go into the water

C

1 If you want to be tall, drink milk every day.
2 Both Kelly and I like to go[going] camping.
3 Either you or Mike should help the teacher.
4 This computer is not only old but also slow. / This computer is slow as well as old.
5 Emma is so sick[ill] that she can't go to school. / Emma can't go to school because she is so sick[ill].
6 I had such a bad toothache that I couldn't eat anything.
7 When I woke up, nobody was[there was nobody] at home.

D

1 1) The steak was so hard that I couldn't eat it.
   2) They gave me such hot soup that I burned my tongue.
2 1) I will buy not only a (baseball) cap but also a (baseball) bat. / I will buy a (baseball) bat as well as a (baseball) cap.
   2) But I will buy neither a baseball glove nor a baseball.

E

1 1) I can use it when I go on a picnic.
   2) I need it because mine is broken.
2 1) I can use them when I play badminton.
   2) I need them because mine are small.

F

1 is cleaning not only the windows but also the floor
2 eat either a sandwich or a hamburger

3 is both listening to music and reading a book

LESSON 3
문장의 확장 II (관계사)

UNIT 1
p. 26~27

A

1 The information which[that] I found on the Internet was useful.

2 I remember the boy who[that] was wearing a shirt with red stripes.

3 You shouldn't forget what I asked you to do.

4 I want to exchange a pair of shoes which[that] are too big for me.

5 The boy who(m)[that] Mr. and Mrs. Miller are looking for is at the playground.

6 This cartoon is what my brother likes most these days.

7 What I want most right now is a glass of water.

B

1 eat smelly food

2 I don't like people who kick other people's seats.

3 I don't like people who talk to their friends loudly.

UNIT 2
p. 27~28

A

1 Julia will visit the company which[that] her father works for.

2 Thomas showed me a photo of a girl who(m)[that] he loved.

3 The hotel which[that] we stayed at was very close to the airport.

4 The book was written in a language which[that] I was not familiar with.

5 I was introduced to the artist who(m)[that] I respect the most.

B

1 1) I went to yesterday was fancy
  2) I ate was terrible

2 1) I bought yesterday was expensive
  2) I took was too old

UNIT 3
p. 28~29

A

1 I can't understand the reason why they laughed at me.

2 October is the month when I was born.

3 Alex asked me the reason why I left without a word.

4 Can you tell me how[the way] you reserved a seat?

5 He will go to the city where he spent his childhood.

B

1 It is the time when my favorite TV show starts.

2 Nobody knows how[the way] she became rich.

3 London is the city where my mother was born.

4 Tell me how[the way] you solved the puzzle.

5 She explained the reason why she couldn't attend the meeting.

6 My uncle showed me the room where he reads books.

7 Erin asked me the reason why I disagreed with her opinion.

WRAP UP
p. 30~32

A

1 I saw a monkey which[that] was peeling a banana.

2 I saw a man who[that] was taking pictures of a tiger.

3 I saw a koala which[that] was climbing the tree.

B

1 Chicken curry is what she is going to make. / Chicken curry is the dish which[that] she is going to make.

2 *Cats* is what she is going to see. / *Cats* is the musical which[that] she is going to see.

3 Jason's house is the place where the party is going to be held.

C

1 Amelia chose a pie which[that] looks delicious.

2 I wore the brown cap (which[that]) my friend bought (for) me.

3 What I need most now is a vacation.

4 The movie is about a boy who[that] wants to be an actor.

5 Robert doesn't know the reason why she is angry at him.

6 My father is looking for the place where he can park his car.

7 We can't believe what he told you.

D

1 1) But what you sent me is something different.
  2) Please send me a red skirt which[that] is one size smaller.

2 1) The department store where the sale was going on was near my house.
  2) I was going to buy a pair of sunglasses (which[that]) I always wanted to have.

4

E

1 1) which offers discounted clothing
   2) Orange Outlet is the place where you can save money!
2 1) which provides unlimited food
   2) Top Kitchen is the place where you can eat as much as you want!

F

1 What I can do well is drawing cartoons.
2 What I can't do well is watercolor painting.
3 What I want to learn is oil painting.

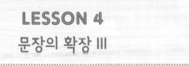

LESSON 4
문장의 확장 III

UNIT 1
p. 34~35

A

1 I wonder if Jamie really likes me.
2 It is true that he is popular at school.
3 I don't know whether he is alive or not.
4 Mike believes that his brother is honest.
5 Our plan is that we will leave tomorrow.
6 Everybody knows that the earth is round.
7 I wonder if I should wear a jacket.
8 It is not certain whether Tom will join us.

B

1 It is not true that Sam stole the wallet.
2 My mother knew that I was telling a lie.
3 He doesn't know whether[if] Lisa is married or not.
4 The fact that you don't like Kate is not important.
5 It is not surprising that Amanda won first prize.
6 I don't know whether[if] David is studying or not.
7 I will check whether[if] the musical is playing now.

C

1 1) It is true that the dog can't run.
   2) I'm sure that it hurt its leg.
2 1) It is surprising that the girl can lift the boxes.
   2) I'm sure that they are empty.

UNIT 2
p. 36~37

A

1 My father bought me a new desk made of wood.
2 Allison bought the dress displayed in the window.
3 The children playing in the playground are my cousins.
4 The helicopter flying over the lake is making a loud noise.

5 The rumor going around the classroom turned out to be false.
6 I know the tall, handsome man standing next to the door.
7 The United Kingdom is a European country surrounded by water.
8 The teacher dressed in blue teaches us science.

B

1 I bought hand cream made in France.
2 I received an email written in English.
3 The dog sitting on the bench is Tom's pet.
4 The twins standing near the tree are cute.
5 The trees planted along the street are tall.
6 The doctor coming out of the hospital is my father.
7 There are many houses built over the water in the country.

C

1 The rose standing in the vase is
2 The boy sitting on the sofa is
3 The dog lying on the floor is

WRAP UP
p. 38~40

A

1 1) The fact that I don't read many books makes me ashamed.
   2) But I am not sure whether[if] I can make time to read.
2 1) The fact that I am always late for school makes me nervous.
   2) But I am not sure whether[if] I can get up early.

B

1 sitting on the bench is reading a book
2 standing by the tall tree is talking on the phone
3 talking to each other are waiting for a bus at the bus stop

C

1 The pool built in the yard is large[big].
2 The boy cooking in the kitchen is Jacob.
3 Sophia is reading a book written in Korean.
4 I wonder whether[if] Ella is at home or not.
5 I agree that we should not use paper cups.
6 It is surprising that the player lost the game.
7 I don't know whether[if] Tracy is a liar or not.

D

1 1) It is surprising that Sean won the dance contest.
   2) I thought that he couldn't participate in the contest.

2 1) The cake decorated with strawberries is my present for her.

2) I wonder whether[if] she will like our presents.

E

1 1) standing in line

2) displayed in the museum

2 1) There were some camels walking across the desert.

2) I entered a large pyramid built with stones.

F

Advantages

1 I think that wearing fashionable clothes gives a good impression.

2 I think that wearing fashionable clothes plays a role in gaining popularity.

Disadvantages

1 I think that following fashion trends costs too much.

2 I think that following fashion trends makes people all look the same.

LESSON 5
문장의 확장 IV

UNIT 1
p. 42~43

A

1 I am not sure who will be my partner.

2 I wonder if[whether] he has a driver's license.

3 I can't remember when Alex's birthday is.

4 I'd like to know if[whether] he finished the project on time.

5 Where do you think they are going to meet?

6 Please tell me how I can get to the subway station.

7 Can you tell me if[whether] you have any plans for this weekend?

B

1 Do you know what time the movie begins?

2 He asked me why I want to be an actor.

3 Laura doesn't know if[whether] there is a drugstore nearby.

4 I didn't know if[whether] she was interested in jazz.

5 My parents asked me if[whether] I wanted to eat out.

6 The man can't remember where he put his wallet.

7 I am not sure when we met for the last time.

8 I wonder how she could get a free coupon.

C

1 if[whether] I had (any) broadcasting experience

2 what skills I had

3 what my dream was

UNIT 2
p. 44~45

A

1 I study at the library for two hours every day.

2 He sat down between Alice and me on the bus.

3 She attached the photo to the wall with tape.

4 I will be at my friend's house this weekend.

5 The shop closes at 5:00 p.m. on Saturdays.

6 Sean will hold a party at his house tonight.

7 They play basketball in the gym after school.

8 He goes to the beach by train during summer vacation.

B

1 My father goes to work on foot every day.

2 She washes the baby with warm water every morning.

3 Bella will leave Seoul by bus next week.

4 Some people are walking along the beach in the afternoon.

5 He borrowed a book from the library near the school.

6 Kevin is staying at the hotel for three days.

7 I saw her running at about 9:00 last night.

C

1 1) Oktoberfest has been held in Germany since 1810.

2) People enjoy it by drinking beer for 16 days.

2 1) The Sapporo Snow Festival has been held in Japan since 1950.

2) People enjoy it by looking at ice sculptures in winter.

WRAP UP
p. 46~48

A

1 We will take a tour around the island by boat at 10:00.

2 We will buy some souvenirs at a traditional market at 13:00.

3 We will leave for the airport by taxi at 15:00.

B

1 1) Please tell me why people have bad eyesight.

2) Also, I wonder what I should do to maintain good eyesight.

2 1) Please tell me why people catch colds.

2) Also, I wonder what I should do to get over a

cold.

C

1 Please tell me where you want to go.
2 The man is hitting the nail with a hammer now.
3 When do you think she will leave for Paris?
4 The boy hid under the desk in the classroom.
5 They gathered in front of the school at 6:00 p.m.
6 Adam can't remember what the man's name is.
7 I wonder if[whether] she has a younger sister.

D

1 1) I was sleeping on the sofa this morning.
   2) She asked me why I didn't go to school.
2 1) Chris was fixing his bike in the yard with a screwdriver yesterday.
   2) He didn't know where his cell phone was.

E

1 He asked me if[whether] you could repair his TV.
2 She asked me if[whether] you could deliver the product.
3 He asked me if[whether] you could send a catalog.

F

1 You can take part in a hot dog eating contest in the cafeteria from 3:00 p.m. to 4:00 p.m.
2 You can play darts at the main entrance from 4:00 p.m. to 4:30 p.m.

SECTION 2
GRAMMAR FOR WRITING

LESSON 6
시제

UNIT 1

p. 52~53

A

1 Your friends are waiting for you.
2 I am watching the show.
3 She speaks French well.
4 Mrs. Jones is cooking spaghetti now. She likes to cook.
5 Evan enjoys going camping. He goes camping five times a year.
6 Water freezes at 0 degrees Celsius and boils at 100 degrees Celsius.
7 I usually go to bed late. But today I am tired, so I am going to bed now.
8 Tom lives alone, but this week he is staying at his parents' house in Philadelphia.
9 It is snowing in Korea now. This is the first time I've seen snow because it doesn't snow in my country.

B

1 1) Miranda usually eats cookies for a snack.
   2) But today, she is eating bananas for a snack.
2 1) Charlie usually plays soccer after school.
   2) But today, he is playing basketball after school.

C

1 1) Kimberly is interested in studying the stars.
   2) So she is looking at the stars[them] through a telescope now.
2 1) Alex is interested in learning to cook.
   2) So he is attending a cooking school now.

UNIT 2

p. 54~55

A

1 I have been here before.
2 He has forgotten it.
3 Nicole has just finished her homework.
4 I saw Olivia on Tuesday. I haven't seen her since then.
5 I bought a book yesterday. But I haven't read it yet.
6 My brother has been sick since last night. So he took medicine this morning.
7 You watched TV too much yesterday, and you have already watched it for two hours today.
8 The author has written a lot of books since 1990, and he received an award last year.

B

1 Andrew bought a pair of shoes. But he hasn't put them on yet.
2 I arrived in Canada last week. I have already visited many places.
3 Joseph has been in London since last year. I sent an email to him yesterday.
4 Emma cut her finger last night. She hasn't washed the dishes since then.
5 I took a Spanish lesson yesterday. But I haven't reviewed it yet.
6 Emily has lost her cell phone. She bought a new one today.

C

1   1) Have you ever played table tennis?

     2) I played two months ago.

     3) I have never played.

2   1) Have you ever played baseball?

     2) I played last month.

     3) I have played twice.

WRAP UP

p. 56~58

A

1   1) She treats animals every day.

     2) But she is playing with a cat now.

2   1) He cuts men's hair every day.

     2) But he is cutting a dog's hair now.

3   1) She practices swimming every day.

     2) But she is playing volleyball now.

B

1   1) Andrew has had a parrot since he was ten years old.

     2) He bought it from a pet shop.

     3) He likes it because it can talk.

2   1) Lillian has had a hamster since she was six years old.

     2) She got it from her friend.

     3) She likes it because it is small and cute.

C

1   The musical began at six and ended at nine.

2   Tony has lived in San Francisco for two years.

3   My cousin has grown taller since I last saw him.

4   I lived in Seoul for ten years, but now I live in New York.

5   Sarah usually wears pants. But today she is wearing a skirt.

6   Emily is doing yoga now because she wants to relieve her stress.

7   My school is far away so I go there by bus.

D

1   1) She is doing a dangerous experiment.

     2) She is being very careful because she doesn't want to make any mistakes.

2   1) I have fixed my computer twice since April.

     2) But it broke again last night.

E

1   1) Until now, I have cleaned my house myself.

     2) But now I'm using a TOP HOUSE Cleaning Robot.

     3) It only needs to be charged, so I can take a rest!

F

1   1) I have been volunteering by teaching Korean to foreigners for three years.

     2) I began doing it to help them feel more comfortable in Korea.

     3) I do it every Saturday at a local library.

LESSON 7
조동사

UNIT 1

p. 60~61

A

1   You had better watch your behavior.

2   I used to play at Jessica's house after school.

3   We had better pay attention to the teacher during classes.

4   I used to like Tom when I was a child.

5   You had better not visit your friends late at night.

6   You had better not tell a lie.

7   I used to keep a diary when I was young.

8   Lauren used to climb mountains with her father on weekends.

B

1   We had better leave now to arrive on time.

2   There used to be many toys in my room when I was young.

3   You had better wear a suit to the interview.

4   Angela used to go snowboarding every winter.

5   You had better not eat too much ice cream.

6   She used to bake bread every Sunday[on Sundays].

7   My grandfather used to grow vegetables in the yard.

8   We had batter not tell her the truth.

C

1   You had better take some medicine.

2   You had better change them.

3   You had better stop playing computer games.

UNIT 2

p. 62~63

A

1   My sister must have worn my skirt.

2   She should have apologized for her mistake.

3   Gwen can't have eaten the chocolate cake.

4   Molly may have given him some candy.

5   They must have seen the car accident.

6   You should have listened to her advice.

7   She may have disagreed with the decision.

8   He can't have forgotten his important appointment.

B

1 Zoe may have been with him yesterday.
2 They must have stolen my backpack.
3 You should have booked a ticket last week.
4 He can't have seen me at the party.
5 She must have heard the sad news.
6 Hunter may have been poor when he was young.
7 John shouldn't have been angry with his mother.

C

1 1) You should have remembered it.
  2) She must have been disappointed.
2 1) You should have been on time.
  2) He must have been bored.

WRAP UP   p. 64~66

A

1 1) I used to stay home every weekend.
  2) I should have done something fun.
2 1) I used to play and sleep too much during vacation.
  2) I should have spent my time more efficiently.

B

1 may have skipped breakfast
2 may have lost her eraser
3 may have walked through some mud

C

1 You had better look at the map.
2 We used to discuss various topics after school.
3 Roy may have been afraid of the dog.
4 Austin can't have accepted their proposal.
5 She must have had a sore throat.
6 You shouldn't have believed the advertisement.
7 You had better not eat too much candy.

D

1 1) But I shouldn't have asked her.
  2) I had better ask my mother to fix it tomorrow.
2 1) Ryan used to buy shoes at a department store.
  2) He should have chosen the size carefully.

E

1 1) escaped in a car
  2) been bald
2 1) He or she must have had bad eyesight.
  2) So he or she may have been old.

F

1 You had better get under the table during an earthquake.
2 You had better not get close to any windows during an earthquake.

UNIT 1   p. 68~69

A

1 He can't decide what to do tomorrow.
2 Peter didn't know where to find the key.
3 Sarah likes to bake bread and cookies.
4 I don't know whom to invite to the party.
5 I found it difficult to take care of babies.
6 Jaeho taught me how to use the machine.
7 Jenny told me when to meet her tomorrow.

D

1 Tell me where to put this box.
2 Hailey learned how to drive a car.
3 They decided who(m) to vote for.
4 Jordan didn't know what to cook for dinner.
5 I want to go to the beach this weekend.
6 To exercise is good for your health.
7 Her plan is to study for the test this weekend.

C

1 1) But he can't decide where to go.
  2) And he doesn't know what to do first.
2 1) But she can't decide who(m) to make it with.
  2) And she doesn't know how to make it.

UNIT 2   p. 70~71

A

1 Ellie needs someone to help her.
2 He went to the store to buy jeans.
3 We went to the cinema to watch a movie.
4 I was glad to get a good score on the test.
5 Julia is too young to understand the book.
6 Chris ran fast enough to catch the bus.
7 There are many attractive places to visit in this city.

B

1 I have good news to tell you.
2 They are looking for a bench to sit on.
3 My cell phone is too big to put in my pocket.
4 My parents were happy to see me dance.
5 Bill went to school on foot to save money.
6 She may be surprised to learn that Debbie is blind.
7 Jim was lucky enough to catch a home run ball.

C

1 1) I once went to the theater to see a play.
  2) I was very amazed to see such a great performance.

2 1) I once went to a tennis court to see a tennis match.
  2) I was very excited to see the great match.

WRAP UP
p. 72~74

A

1 Did he decide when to go there?

2 Did he decide how to go there?

3 Did he decide who(m) to go there with?

B

1 1) to express my feelings
  2) to see Jim's[his] friends eat it

2 1) to give to my parents
  2) to see the pretty house

C

1 The racehorse is too old to run in the race.

2 I forgot what to say in front of the audience.

3 I am looking for someone to ask for directions.

4 His plan is to make a movie about true friendship.

5 Alicia doesn't know how to thank him for the gift[present].

6 The people stood up to see the shooting stars better.

7 I was surprised to hear the score of the baseball game.

D

1 1) He didn't know who(m) to ask for help.
  2) She told him how to get to the hotel.

2 1) I started doing it because I wanted to lose weight.
  2) I am happy to find a way to relax.

E

1 1) I don't know how to get there.
  2) I don't know what (present) to buy him, either.

F

Advantages

1 1) difficult enough to make you responsible
  2) take care of pets to learn to be responsible

Disadvantages

1 1) too smelly to play with
  2) wash them often to make them smell better

LESSON 9
비교급과 최상급

UNIT 1
p. 76~77

A

1 Ian eats twice as much as me.

2 He is getting taller and taller these days.

3 The more I sleep, the more tired I feel.

4 The later he comes, the angrier she is.

5 More and more students are using smartphones.

6 My father is three times heavier than my sister.

7 Amy can remember names as well as I can.

B

1 Bailey is getting[becoming] more and more beautiful.

2 My cat is getting[becoming] heavier and heavier.

3 The hotel room was twice as large as my room.

4 Her parents are as strict as my parents.

5 This problem is ten times more complicated than[as complicated as] that one.

6 I am as worried as Evan about the test.

7 The harder you study, the better your grade will be.

8 The younger children are, the more attention they need.

C

1 Zoe couldn't run as well as Sophia.
Sophia ran twice as fast as Zoe.

2 Tony couldn't jump as well as Ryan.
Ryan jumped three times as far as Tony.

UNIT 2
p. 78~79

A

1 Yesterday was the happiest day of my life.

2 John is the tallest boy in his class.

3 He is one of the laziest students in my class.

4 This car is more comfortable than all the other cars.

5 This dish is more delicious than any other dish in the restaurant.

6 Sarah is one of the kindest nurses in the hospital.

7 A hurricane is more dangerous than any other kind of storm.

8 This scene is more exciting than any other part of this movie.

B

1 January is the coldest month of the year.
2 Mrs. Wood is more popular than all the other teachers.
3 This sweater looks warmer than any other sweater in the store.
4 He is one of the most attractive actors in Korea.
5 Her desk is dirtier than any other desk in the classroom.
6 Jack Sparrow is one of the most unique characters in the movie.
7 She has the most beautiful voice in my class.
8 These slippers are cheaper than all the other shoes in the store.

C

1 This dress is more stylish than all the other dresses here.
2 This coat is warmer than all the other coats here.
3 This hat is cuter than all the other hats here.

WRAP UP

p. 80~82

A

1 is twice as expensive as DG487
2 is three times as heavy as DG487
3 is three times as thick as DG487
4 storage capacity is as big as DG487's

B

1 1) She is one of the most respected women in the world.
  2) I think she was more generous than any other person.
2 1) He is one of the most popular movie stars in the world.
  2) I think he is more handsome than any other actor.

C

1 The sound of the rain is getting[becoming] louder and louder.
2 The more places you travel, the more experiences you will have.
3 The Yangtze River is longer than any other river in China.
4 Sirius is the brightest star in the night sky.
5 Blake is more cheerful than all the other boys in the town.
6 This month, I spent twice as much money as last month.
7 He is one of the funniest comedians in the U.S.

D

1 1) Kimberly is prettier than any other girl in my class.

  2) The hole seemed to be getting[becoming] bigger and bigger.
2 1) It is one of the most fashionable bags these days.
  2) It was three times as cheap as[cheaper than] mine.

E

1 1) People are reading less and less.
  2) The more you read, the more intelligent you can be!

F

1 The club has more useful discussions than any other club in our school.
2 The club does more creative activities than any other club in our school.

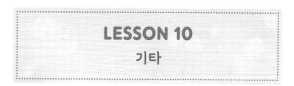

LESSON 10
기타

UNIT 1

p. 84~85

A

1 I will have John cook dinner.
2 I have taken five exams so far.
3 I have not cleaned my room yet.
4 Dylan had the wall painted blue.
5 My mother had a cup of coffee this morning.
6 My grandfather had me read a book to him.
7 We had a nice time in Singapore during summer vacation.

B

1 My father had Kevin take my picture.
2 We have known each other for five years.
3 My family has never been to England before.
4 My teacher had me read the book in English class.
5 Grace had a chicken sandwich and orange juice for lunch.
6 He had many friends before he transferred to this school.
7 Have you ever bought clothes on the Internet at a cheap price?

C

1 1) Our teacher had us avoid wasting electricity.
  2) Since then, we have turned off the lights
2 1) Our teacher had us avoid wasting energy.
  2) Since then, we have worn long underwear

UNIT 2

p. 86~87

A

1 Each person in the station looks tired.
2 Not everyone will come to the wedding.
3 His jokes do not always make us laugh.
4 Walking five miles every day is not easy.
5 She is not in the classroom but in the library.
6 A number of people are watching the game.
7 He enjoys climbing mountains and fishing.

B

1 Not all of us agree with his opinion.
2 The number of students in my school is increasing.
3 Emma goes to school by bus or on foot.
4 Booking plane tickets to New York was difficult.
5 Joseph does not always go to church on Sundays.
6 Each student has an opportunity to attend the program.
7 Mike likes watching[to watch] TV and playing[to play] soccer.

C

1 1) Wearing a school uniform is required.
  2) But not all the students are wearing one.
2 1) Dancing to music is fun.
  2) But not all the students enjoy it.

WRAP UP

p. 88~90

A

1 I have a friend who likes to make cakes. She has made 10 cakes so far.
2 I have a friend who likes to write novels. He has written 15 novels so far.
3 I have a friend who likes to see plays. She has seen 12 plays so far.

B

1 1) But not every towel is soft.
  2) And each towel is dirty.
2 1) But not all the umbrellas are big.
  2) And every umbrella has a hole in it.

C

1 John has many books, but he doesn't read them.
2 The singer has had concerts in many cities around the world.
3 I like the song not because of its melody but because of its lyrics.
4 Walking in the woods makes me feel good.
5 A number of mice are used in experiments every year.
6 The firefighter had the children cover their noses and mouths with wet towels.
7 Not every student wants[Not all the students want] to take part in the talent show.

D

1 1) I have lived in this house since last year.
  2) It has a beautiful balcony where I can see the river.
2 1) But taking care of a dog is not easy.
  2) You have to feed, walk, and wash it.
  3) But not everyone likes dogs.

E

1 1) I like the book a lot, so I have read it twice.
  2) Read this book and have an exciting experience!
2 1) I like the book a lot, so I have read it four times.
  2) Read this book and have faith in your dreams!

F

1 not everyone can
2 you must peel and eat two shrimp
3 using two hands is

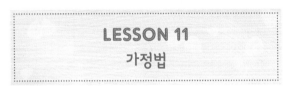

LESSON 11
가정법

UNIT 1

p. 92~93

A

1 If it weren't snowing heavily, we could climb the mountain.
2 If I didn't have a headache, I could run in the marathon.
3 If he saved money, he could buy a new headset.
4 If that store were open on Sundays, I would not have to find another one.
5 If she had a camera, she would not have to borrow one.
6 If he knew the route, he would not be confused.
7 If they didn't run around the classroom, I could focus on my studies.
8 If you were not busy, you could spend time with your family.

B

1 If I could be born again, I would become a doctor.
2 If I were not sleepy, I could see the movie.
3 If the singer had a concert, I would buy a ticket.
4 If Lisa lived near my house, we would meet every day.

5 If it didn't rain, we could have dinner in the garden.
6 If Brandon knew her phone number, he would call her.

C

1 1) If I were a wizard, I would ride on a magic broom.
   2) If I were a wizard, I would change into a bird.
2 1) If I explored the North Pole, I would see polar bears.
   2) If I explored the North Pole, I would make an igloo.

UNIT 2
p. 94~95

A

1 I wish Sam listened to others' opinions.
2 I wish I were good at singing.
3 I wish I had a sister to play with.
4 I wish I could remember his name.
5 as if he were the president of the club
6 as if they knew the suspect
7 as if she could solve the problem
8 as if she were my teacher

B

1 I wish you could speak French.
2 I wish I were taller than my brother.
3 I wish my father worked for a game company.
4 Ellie acts[behaves] as if she had a lot of work.
5 I wish I could visit my grandmother's house.
6 He talks[speaks] as if I were jealous of him.
7 Mrs. Brown treats me as if I were her daughter.

C

1 1) I wish I could swim in the pool with you.
   2) He acts as if he had no time.
2 1) I wish I could read books in the library with you.
   2) She acts as if she were a baby.

WRAP UP
p. 96~98

A

1 as if she were a student
2 as if he were flying in the sky
3 as if he were jumping rope
4 as if she were a model

B

1 I wish I could save money.
2 I wish I could learn how to dance.
3 I wish I could do some volunteer work.
4 I wish I could buy more clothes.

C

1 If I bought new shoes, I could run fast.
2 If I lived in Busan, I would swim in the sea every day.
3 I wish I could travel around the world.
4 If today were Sunday, I wouldn't go to school.
5 Gina spends money as if she were rich.
6 I wish I had a handsome boyfriend.

D

1 1) If she came home early, my parents wouldn't worry about her.
   2) I wish she kept her promises.
2 1) If I went to Sydney, we could go to the Opera House together.
   2) I wish I could go to school with you.

E

1 1) as if he were a rock singer
   2) If I were you, I would use earplugs.
2 1) as if I got a text message
   2) If I were you, I would turn off my phone for a while.

F

1 1) If I could travel to the past, I would go to the Jurassic age.
   2) I wish I could see real dinosaurs.
2 1) If I could travel to the past, I would go to the Joseon Dynasty.
   2) I wish I could meet King Sejong.

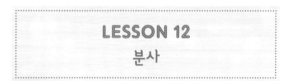

LESSON 12
분사

UNIT 1
p. 100~101

A

1 Seeing me, she ran away.
2 Walking to school, Robert was talking with his friend.
3 Taking a walk, Anne talked on the phone.
4 Eating breakfast, Christine read the newspaper.
5 Visiting their website, you can find more information.
6 Cooking dinner, Ashley heard the doorbell ring.
7 Setting the table, he sang his favorite song.
8 Staying at my uncle's house, I finished the book.
9 Joining the book club, you must read a lot of books.

B

1 Swinging her arms, Lily danced on the stage.

2 Turning left, you will see the flower shop.

3 Feeling tired, I went to bed early.

4 Opening the door, Lauren looked around the classroom.

5 Hearing the news, John jumped with joy.

6 Listening to the radio, I studied math.

7 Turning on my cell phone, I checked the text messages.

C

1 1) Carrying a bag, Justin is talking on the phone.
   2) Talking on the phone, Justin is running to school.

2 1) Waiting for a bus, Michelle is listening to music.
   2) Listening to music, Michelle is eating a hamburger.

UNIT 2
p. 102~103

A

1 The bird flew away with its leg broken.

2 Morgan ate a hamburger with her baby sleeping beside her.

3 Paul left home with the windows open.

4 Alex talked to his teacher with his hands in his pockets.

5 With night coming on, it became dark.

6 Seven dogs were born with their eyes closed.

7 With the snow falling hard, Ted didn't go out.

8 The monkey was hanging on the tree with its legs swinging.

B

1 John came to school with his hair cut.

2 Eat the cookies with your mouth closed.

3 Daniel fell asleep with his legs crossed.

4 Julia was running with her dog following her.

5 Emily waited for David with her heart beating fast.

6 Bill came home with his right arm broken.

7 The book was displayed with some pages missing.

C

1 is lying with its legs crossed

2 is eating leaves with its eyes closed

3 is swimming with its mouth open

WRAP UP
p. 104~106

A

1 1) the computer on

2 1) Eating lunch
   2) "Don't speak with your mouth full."

3 1) Wearing his shoes
   2) "Don't walk around the house with your shoes on."

B

1 Walking down the street, Susie[she] found a cat.

2 Coming up to Susie[her], the cat cried.

3 Carrying the cat, Susie[she] returned home.

C

1 Walking along the street, I met my English teacher.

2 Taylor fell asleep with the TV on last night.

3 Sitting in a chair, she read a fashion magazine.

4 She blew out the candles with her eyes closed.

5 Passing by my house, Pamela called my name.

6 Ben was sitting on the sofa with his legs crossed.

7 Feeling tired, Sam did not go to the airport to see his brother off.

D

1 1) Singing a song, he mixed them together.
   2) Eating a spoonful of *bibimbap*, he frowned.

2 1) Giving her a ring, he proposed to her.
   2) With tears in her eyes, she accepted the ring.

E

1 did an amazing spin holding one ankle above her head

2 attempting a triple jump, she fell down

3 she stood up and glided gracefully with a smile on her face

F

1 Taking a woman's bag

2 Running after the thief, a man caught him.

3 Getting her bag back, the woman thanked the man.

SECTION 3
PATTERNS FOR WRITING

Useful Patterns for Writing 1

1 Being friends means trusting each other.

2 Please let me go with you.

3 A broken mirror means bad luck in many cultures.

4 Please let me use your cell phone.

5 Being an adult means taking responsibility for your actions.
6 Please let me know your email address.
7 Success doesn't mean earning a lot of money.
8 Please let me explain my situation.
9 Red means fortune and good luck to the Chinese.
10 Please let me know your final decision.

Useful Patterns for Writing 2

1 In this sentence, "it" refers to global warming.
2 I am sure[certain] that our team will win this game.
3 These figures refer to the number of students in each school
4 I am quite[fairly] sure[certain] that he will apologize soon.
5 The word "vegetarian" refers to a person who does not eat meat.
6 I am not sure[certain] if I can finish this essay today.
7 What does the underlined sentence refer to?
8 I am absolutely sure[certain] that she will come back soon.
9 The term "biology" refers to the study of living things.
10 I am not quite sure[certain] if he studied for the test.

Useful Patterns for Writing 3

1 In my opinion, he is wasting his time.
2 Language can be defined as a system of communication.
3 In my opinion, you are responsible for the failure.
4 A family is defined as a group of people who are related to each other.
5 In my opinion, he made a serious mistake.
6 A hobby is defined as an activity (which[that]) people regularly do for pleasure.
7 In my opinion, the rumors about her are not true.
8 A green job can be defined as a job which[that] protects the environment.
9 In my opinion, computers make our lives more complex.
10 Using another person's ID can be defined as theft.

Useful Patterns for Writing 4

1 I wonder if I could use your computer.
2 It seems to me that no one lives in that old house.
3 I wonder if you could teach me math.
4 It seems to me that you don't believe me anymore.
5 I wonder if you could help me move this chair.
6 It seems to me that the thief was not a man.
7 I wonder if I could ask you some questions.
8 It seems to me that he is a good baseball player.
9 I wonder if you could take me home now.
10 It seems to me that the president is very popular.

Useful Patterns for Writing 5

1 I really appreciate your kind reply to my question.
2 I apologize for the inconvenience this may cause.
3 We appreciate your interest in our club.
4 I apologize for what I said to you this morning.
5 I appreciate your understanding in this matter.
6 We apologize for the late arrival of the bus.
7 We appreciate your time and effort.
8 I apologize for the delay in answering your letter.
9 I appreciate your help in making this website.
10 I apologize for keeping you waiting outside.

Useful Patterns for Writing 6

1 I like to spend time surfing the Internet.
2 You are wasting your time choosing clothes to wear.
3 He spent most of his money remodeling his house.
4 He wasted a lot of time hanging around with Jim.
5 I spend most of my time exercising these days.
6 I wasted money watching a boring movie.
7 They want to spend more money advertising the product.
8 We wasted time waiting for a taxi yesterday.
9 She spends her spare time taking care of flowers.
10 I don't want to waste money buying pens (which[that]) I won't use.

Useful Patterns for Writing 7

1 I would rather take a taxi than (take a) crowded bus.
2 I could not help agreeing with his decision.
3 I would rather do it alone than ask for your help.
4 I cannot help hiding my true feelings about her.
5 I would rather sleep than read a boring book.

6 We could not help admitting our mistake.

7 I would rather sing a song than dance.

8 When I see chocolate, I cannot help eating it.

9 I would rather be cold than wear that old jacket.

10 I could not help respecting his passion for movies.

Useful Patterns for Writing 8

1 They know how to solve the environmental problem.

2 He is anxious to live in a quiet place.

3 I know how to lose weight in a healthy way.

4 She is anxious to have her own room.

5 He knows how to give a good first impression.

6 I am anxious to travel around the world with my family.

7 She knows how to make her parents happy.

8 We are anxious to know who will teach us.

9 I don't know how to play this game.

10 They are anxious to get to the airport on time.

Useful Patterns for Writing 9

1 He is as strong as any athlete that has ever played.

2 I can no longer stand his rude behavior. / I can't stand his rude behavior any longer.

3 She is as good[great] as any artist that has ever lived.

4 People are no longer allowed to smoke in public places. / People are not allowed to smoke in public places any longer.

5 She is as honest as any politician that has ever lived.

6 The company no longer wants to produce sports cars. / The company doesn't want to produce sports cars any longer.

7 He is as talented as any tennis player that has ever played.

8 He no longer wants to fight with his brother. / He doesn't want to fight with his brother any longer.

9 The song is as good[great] as any song that has ever been sung.

10 She no longer cares about other people's opinions. / She doesn't care about other people's opinions any longer.

Useful Patterns for Writing 10

1 He is the most successful person I have ever met.

2 We had a hard time deciding what to eat for lunch.

3 This fantasy novel is the most boring book I have ever read.

4 He had a hard time finding the bakery yesterday.

5 This is the most delicious fried rice I have ever tasted.

6 I am having a hard time understanding the lecture.

7 This musical is the greatest performance I have ever seen.

8 She is having a hard time setting up her blog.

9 This trip will be the most valuable experience we have ever had.

10 They had a hard time catching a taxi.

Useful Patterns for Writing 11

1 If I were you, I would go to bed early.

2 If it were not for the test, I would not feel stressed.

3 If I were you, I would never give up hope.

4 If it were not for the Internet, our lives would be very different.

5 If I were you, I would drive more slowly at night.

6 If it were not for the rain, we could enjoy our trip.

7 If I were you, I would not stay in such an expensive hotel.

8 If it were not for ovens, I could not bake bread.

9 If I were you, I would consult with my teacher.

10 If it were not for my friends, I would feel lonely sometimes.

Useful Patterns for Writing 12

1 I told her not to worry about her test score.

2 It is probable[likely] that more tourists will visit the country next year.

3 He told me not to bring my pet to his house.

4 It is not possible to climb the mountain in this bad weather.

5 I told her not to invite Jake to the Christmas party.

6 It is probable[likely] that she will win the flute competition.

7 She told us not to touch the important document.

8 It is possible to change your decision now.

9 I told her not to apologize to me for the mistake.

10 It is probable[likely] that they will announce the results of the experiment soon.

교과서 필수 문법으로 익히는 영어 문장 쓰기

WRITING BUILDER 3

www.nebooks.co.kr

NE 능률

기복 없는 단단한 영어 실력, 서술형을 잡아라!

최신 중간·기말고사
빈출 서술형 마스터

쓰기로
마스터하는
중학서술형

3학년

NE능률 영어교육연구소 지음
신유승 선정아 강동효 은다나

NE 능률

전국 **온오프 서점** 판매중

내신 빈출 문제로 서술형 실력 완성 쓰마중

1학년
(예비중-중1)

2학년
(중2)

3학년
(중3)

실전 내신 대비가 가능한 양질의 문제 수록

· 중학 교과서 및 전국의 최신 내신 시험지 분석, 반영
· 기출 응용문제 및 누적 TEST 제공

표준 서술형 유형부터 빈출 유형까지 완벽 대비

· 필수 문법 항목, 문장 쓰기 연습을 단계별로 학습
· 서술형 빈출 유형별 문제 풀이 과정 제시

NE능률 교재 MAP

아래 교재 MAP을 참고하여 본인의 현재 혹은 목표 수준에 따라 교재를 선택하세요.
NE능률 교재들과 함께 영어실력을 쑥쑥~ 올려보세요!
MP3 등 교재 부가 학습 서비스 및 자세한 교재 정보는 www.nebooks.co.kr 에서 확인하세요.

문법구문

초1-2	초3	초3-4	초4-5	초5-6
	그래머버디 1 초등영어 문법이 된다 Starter 1	그래머버디 2 초등영어 문법이 된다 Starter 2 초등 Grammar Inside 1 초등 Grammar Inside 2	그래머버디 3 Grammar Bean 1 Grammar Bean 2 초등영어 문법이 된다 1 초등 Grammar Inside 3 초등 Grammar Inside 4	Grammar Bean 3 Grammar Bean 4 초등영어 문법이 된다 2 초등 Grammar Inside 5 초등 Grammar Inside 6

초6-예비중	중1	중1-2	중2-3	중3
능률중학영어 예비중 Grammar Inside Starter 원리를 더한 영문법 STARTER	능률중학영어 중1 Grammar Zone 입문편 Grammar Zone 워크북 입문편 1316팬클럽 문법 1 문제로 마스터하는 중학영문법 1 Grammar Inside 1 열중 16강 문법 1 쓰기로 마스터하는 중학서술형 1학년	능률중학영어 중2 1316팬클럽 문법 2 문제로 마스터하는 중학영문법 2 Grammar Inside 2 열중 16강 문법 2 고득점 독해를 위한 중학 구문 마스터 1 원리를 더한 영문법 1 중학영문법 총정리 모의고사 1	Grammar Zone 기초편 Grammar Zone 워크북 기초편 고득점 독해를 위한 중학 구문 마스터 2 원리를 더한 영문법 2 중학영문법 총정리 모의고사 2 쓰기로 마스터하는 중학서술형 2학년 천문장 입문	능률중학영어 중3 1316팬클럽 문법 3 문제로 마스터하는 중학영문법 3 Grammar Inside 3 열중 16강 문법 3 고득점 독해를 위한 중학 구문 마스터 3 중학영문법 총정리 모의고사 3 쓰기로 마스터하는 중학서술형 3학년

예비고-고1	고1	고1-2	고2-3	고3
문제로 마스터하는 고등영문법 올클 수능 어법 start 천문장 기본	Grammar Zone 기본편 1 Grammar Zone 워크북 기본편 1 Grammar Zone 기본편 2 Grammar Zone 워크북 기본편 2 필히 통하는 고등영문법 기본	필히 통하는 고등영문법 실력편 TEPS BY STEP G+R Basic	Grammar Zone 종합편 Grammar Zone 워크북 종합편 올클 수능 어법 완성 천문장 완성	

수능 이상/ 토플 80-89 · 텝스 600-699점	수능 이상/ 토플 90-99 · 텝스 700-799점	수능 이상/ 토플 100 · 텝스 800점 이상		
TEPS BY STEP G+R 1	TEPS BY STEP G+R 2	TEPS BY STEP G+R 3		

10분 만에 끝내는 영어 수업 준비!

NETutor

NE Tutor는 NE능률이 만든 대한민국 대표 **영어 티칭 플랫폼**으로
영어 수업에 필요한 **모든 콘텐츠와 서비스**를 제공합니다.

www.netutor.co.kr

· 전국 영어 학원 선생님들이 뽑은 NE Tutor 서비스 TOP 3! ·

1st. 스마트 문제뱅크 1분이면 맞춤형 어휘, 문법 테스트지 완성!!
문법, 독해, 어휘 추가 문제 출제 가능

2nd. 레벨테스트 학부모 상담 시 필수 아이템!!
초등 1학년부터 중등 3학년까지 9단계 학생 수준 진단

3rd. E-Book 이젠 연구용 교재 없이도 모든 책 내용을 볼 수 있다!!
ELT부터 중고등까지 온라인 수업 교재로 활용

NE_Tutor

Got A Book For Vocabulary?

" The Original and The Best "

Here is the **No.1 vocabulary book** in Korea, recognized by more teachers and used by more students than any other vocabulary book ever made. **Get yours today!** You won't regret it!

SINCE 1983

Korea's NO. 1 Vocabulary Book